INFORMAL DIAGNOSTIC ASSESSMENT OF CHILDREN

INFORMAL DIAGNOSTIC
ASSESSMENT
OF CHILDREN

By

THEODORE S. FREMONT, Ed.D.

Assistant Professor of Educational Psychology
Wichita State University
Wichita, Kansas

DAVID M. SEIFERT, Ed.D.

Pediatric Psychologist
Wichita Guidance Center
Wichita, Kansas

JOHN H. WILSON, Ed.D.

Associate Professor of Elementary Education
Wichita State University
Wichita, Kansas

CHARLES C THOMAS · PUBLISHER
Springfield · Illinois · U.S.A.

Published and Distributed Throughout the World by

Bannerstone House

301-327 East Lawrence Avenue, Springfield, Illinois, U.S.A.

© *1977, by* CHARLES C THOMAS • PUBLISHER

ISBN 0-398-03646-2

Library of Congress Catalog Card Number 76-30447

Library of Congress Cataloging in Publication Data

Fremont, Theodore S.
    Informal diagnostic assessment of children.

    Bibliography: p.
    Includes index.
    1. Learning disabilities. 2. Minimal brain dysfunc-
tion in children. I. Seifert, David M., joint author.
II. Wilson, John Harold, 1935-   joint author.
III. Title. [DNLM: 1. Child behavior disorders—
Diagnosis. 2. Child development deviations—Diagnosis.
3. Learning disorders—Diagnosis. WS350 F872i]
LC4704.F73   371.9   76-30447
ISBN 0-398-03646-2

Printed in the United States of America

C-1

Dedication

To THE MANY children who deserve to be identified for their unique exceptionalities and ac-
cepted while intelligent referral procedures are set
in motion.

To the many teachers and others who are concerned about the ultimate welfare of young learners—those teachers who are willing to seek out the
talents of professionals with particular skills and
similar concerns.

Preface

EDUCATORS ARE BECOMING increasingly aware of exceptionalities in education including the learning disabled, the mentally retarded, the neurological- and health-impaired, and the emotionally disturbed. Because teachers have routine and consistent contact with children on a daily basis, they are in the best position to recognize and identify actual or potential behavioral, learning, and psychological disorders. If childhood disorders, whether obvious or masked, are not recognized within the school atmosphere and parents have not previously identified them, it is unlikely that their identification will become realized until the child is older, when the prognosis for improvement is more guarded. Without early identification and subsequent treatment, these difficulties can increase in intensity, develop into additional symptoms, result in frustration and despondency, and interfere with social and academic performance. A remediation program, whether for psychological difficulties, behavioral disorders, learning problems, or brain dysfunctions, can be implemented once the problems have been identified. As more teachers become educated observers of behavior, the probability of children passing through elementary school with psychological and learning difficulties will be minimized.

Informal Diagnostic Assessment of Children was developed with the purpose of delineating diagnostic techniques for recognizing children who are experiencing psychological and educational deficits. It was not written with the intent to label children with a diagnostic nomenclature. The diagnostic methods introduced in this volume are presented so that a child who is experiencing problems can be identified without the use of formal psychological or educational testing devices. The authors do not discourage formal psychological and educational testing but encourage informal assessment for initial evaluation and identification of childhood disorders. With increased use of *Informal Diagnostic Assessment of Children,* a greater number of youngsters with problems can be identified and referred for a more intense and complete formal workup. Thus, informal assessment will provide the information necessary to facilitate special educational placement or make referral to other school or community resources and will provide a psychologically based communication system for school personnel.

Using this approach, teachers are educated and equipped to become familiar with the symptoms which would normally need further evaluation on a formal or informal basis by a mental health specialist. Their role should be that of skilled observer and recorder, one who gathers pertinent information about children who may have special needs. Teachers cannot and should not be expected to remediate the problems described in this book. They are not psychotherapists, neurologists, or school psychologists. However, the authors maintain that teachers have the greatest opportunity to objectively and comparatively describe children with whom they spend up to 7 hours daily, 180 days yearly. Teachers have too long been given too little credit for their ability to act as resource people for other specialists. They have also been undertrained to act in this special capacity. This book attempts to help fill that gap, to make use of this extensive body of experts—classroom teachers.

Informal Diagnostic Assessment of Children makes use of those techniques which child psychologists and some school mental health specialists use in their diagnostic evaluation of children. Because the informal assessment stresses recognition through observation, it not only facilitates the referral for diagnostic evaluation by a specialist (physician, psychologist, etc.) but it offers the teacher a strong basis upon which to make a helpful referral.

The approach suggested in this text familarizes teachers with developmental deviations, brain disorders, learning problems, and emotional status of children, while the process offers a language system which facilitates communication with mental health and educational specialists. The language is common to clinical psychologists, child psychiatrists, and school mental health specialists. *Informal Diagnostic Assessment of Children* is designed to be especially helpful to elementary school classroom teachers and also useful for other individuals interested in learning how to recognize children with learning problems. Particular areas of this volume will provide resource information for other specialists including nurses, special educators, and resource people.

The manuscript is divided into four major chapters. These chapters include classroom evaluation, developmental history, brain dysfunctions, and emotional evaluation. The first chapter, Classroom Evaluation, provides information necessary for identifying children who exhibit problems within the classroom environment. Both behavioral and academic disorders are delineated and may be more readily recognized by following the suggestions given in this part of the text. The second chapter, Developmental History, explores all the developmental and neurological milestones of the child prior to age five. While this chapter may seem less relevant to the needs of the classroom teacher (since the information given here must come largely from the parent), it is of great importance when making a determination about the onset and etiology of the disorder. Therefore, the teacher should obtain early developmental history from the parent when its importance is suggested. By having a complete and accurate understanding of the child's developmental background, a more thorough evaluation of a child's present problem will be enhanced. The third chapter, Brain Dysfunctions, explores those very subtle indicators which suggest neurological and perceptual dysfunctions. It is often the case that children experiencing brain dysfunctions are wrongly treated for emotional disorders. Thus, it is essential that symptoms which relate to brain dysfunctions be analyzed before any attempt is made to characterize the emotional status of the child. The fourth chapter, Emotional Evaluation, supplies the reader with extensive information that is necessary for assessing a variety of psychological disorders.

The authors are aware that all psychological and educational problems are not presented in this volume; instead, an attempt was made to include the most common disorders. The reader is advised to follow the sequence of the chapters as presented in this volume. As one becomes more familiar with the evaluation process, however, specializing in one or more areas may be more appropriate. It is generally recommended that a teacher be quite well acquainted with a child (usually well into the first semester) before s/he completes the informal assessment that is outlined herein. Also, some of the language and terminology may be unfamiliar to the reader; thus, a glossary has been provided at the end of the book.

Introduction

INFORMAL DIAGNOSTIC ASSESSMENT OF CHILDREN is designed to provide teachers with the necessary skills to identify children who are in need of specialized assistance. This approach not only emphasizes the obvious learning and behavioral disorders but also those which are subtle or masked and difficult to recognize. It supplies the teacher with a solid basis by which to make comparison judgements of learning and behavioral disorders and to discriminate healthy from unhealthy behavior. The emphasis of the informal approach is on the observation of behavior by a means that Carl Rogers would label as the participant observer. The participant is the teacher interacting with children, and the observer is the teacher monitoring and studying the behavior of these youngsters. This approach formalizes the teacher's role as a diagnostician of learning and behavioral disorders.

It is not the aim of *Informal Diagnostic Assessment of Children* to supply teachers and other professionals with diagnoses by which to categorize children. Although the emphasis is on recognition of behavioral and learning problems, it is important not to label the child or "psychologize" about the rationale for the child's difficulties. It must be recalled that Freud said that the best diagnosis comes after treatment and not subsequent to it. Thus, rather than labeling children, it is more important to identify the behavioral and learning attributes by frequency and duration and provide a functional definition for the disorder when appropriate. Labeling children for the sake of labeling children and subsequently placing them in a category does not serve the best interests of the child. The informal assessment attempts to provide teachers and professionals with a sensitivity by which they can identify children who are experiencing significant difficulties. Thus, these children may be referred to other specialists for a more in-depth evaluation and assessment. By following the suggestions outlined in this volume, there should be little question by the professional regarding the rationale for the child being nominated for a more formal evaluation. In some cases, it might be that the child is recommended for psychological counseling or psychotherapy, and in other cases, the child may be recommended for special education placement. Regardless of the final remediation suggestion, it is essential that teachers become acquainted and familiarized with the various subtle and overt behavioral and learning differences of children.

There are four suggested guidelines which are consistent with the informal diagnostic assessment for referring a child for specialized assessment and/or treatment. A teacher should refer the child who is experiencing one condition or a number of the conditions indicated:

1. If the symptom is frequently manifesting itself with a great deal of intensity;
2. If the symptom is interfering with ongoing academic performance, intellectual functioning, cognitive activity, emotional functions, and social interactions;
3. If there is a variety of different symptoms evolving, and/or
4. If the child indicates a need for special assistance.

Once the teacher has determined that a child is in need of more specialized assistance than can be handled in the classroom, a referral to a specialist is appropriate. The teacher considering a referral should keep in mind that (1) the procedure for implementing such a referral must be consistent with the school's guidelines, (2) care must be taken to not alienate parents when relating the symptoms of children, (3) the teacher should work closely with the guidance counselor and school psychologist, as well as the principal, in implementing and suggesting the referral, (4) usually the child may not be referred without parental permission, (5) it is important when relating information on a child that the teacher talk in behavioral and objective terms so that there is no dispute about the identification of the symptoms, and (6) the teacher should constantly make comparisons with other children of the same chronological age and grade.

The following is a list of specialists who are useful in dealing with problems of children.

Audiologist: A specialist who concentrates on the diagnosis, treatment, and rehabilitation of persons with impaired hearing.

Clinical Child Psychologist: A professional who has a Ph.D., Ed.D., or Psy.D. degree and is qualified to evaluate and remediate psychological disorders. Clinical psychologists should be licensed or certified by the state in which they practice.

Educational Psychologist: A professional who has a Ph.D. or Ed.D. degree and specializes in the application of psychological principles to the educational environment. Some educational psychologists will consult on classroom learning styles, motivation, and educational testing practices.

Educational Strategist: An education specialist who concentrates on the recognition and remediation of learning problems and assists teachers in implementing procedures for the needs of handicapped students. The strategist should be certified by the State Board of Education, Department of Special Education, for the state in which s/he is employed.

Neurologist: A physician who specializes in the diagnosis and treatment of diseases affecting the nervous system. The medical practitioner should be licensed under state law.

Ophthalmologist: A physician who specializes with the anatomy, functions, and diseases of the eye. This specialist also prescribes corrective lenses. The medical practitioner should be licensed under state law.

Optometrist: A specialist who tests the eyes for defects of vision in order to prescribe corrective lenses. These professionals are primarily diagnosticians of eye disorders and will refer to the ophthalmologist when medical pathology is suspected.

Pediatrician: A medical specialist who concentrates on the development and treatment of childhood diseases through age fourteen. The medical practitioner should be licensed under state law.

Psychiatric Social Worker: A professional who usually has a Master's degree in Social Work (MSW) and specializes in individual and family treatment of problems in living. In some states they are licensed/certified by the state, and in others they are licensed through their state organization.

School Social Worker: A professional employed with the school system who specializes in the home and family constellation as they affect the elementary school-age child. School social workers are usually certified through the State Board of Education by the state in which they are employed.

School Mental Health Specialists:

SCHOOL PSYCHOLOGIST—a school staff member with specialized training in psychological and educational procedures and techniques (preferably holding at least an M.A. degree in psychology or educational psychology). The psychologist performs group and individual psychological and educational evaluations and consults with children, parents, teachers, and other professional workers in the school and in the community. Recent legislation in many states mandates school psychologists to implement special education placements.

GUIDANCE COUNSELOR—one who assists individual students to make adjustments and choices in regard to vocational, educational, and personal matters and/or counsels on psychological problems.

The primary goal of the informal diagnostic assessment of the elementary school-age child is for the teacher to become a more sophisticated diagnostician of learning and behavior disorders of children. Through this approach, more children can be reached, especially those with subtle and difficult-to-recognize disorders. Once these children are identified and, if need be, referred for a more intensive evaluation, then a remediation program can be established to facilitate the child's adjustment to family, peers, school, and/or self.

Acknowledgements

THE DEVELOPMENT of the text has been supported by many un-identified sources, people, and materials deserving of recognition because of their subtle contributions to this work. We do want to especially recognize the input of Ms. Eunice Nelson, an assistant professor in the field of exceptionalities, who helped us with several sections of the text. We are, indeed, indebted to her for carefully reviewing much of the technical advice included here. Also, we want to thank Ms. Bonnie Hanson, an elementary classroom teacher, who reviewed all of the manuscript in its formative stages. As a result of her suggestions, we feel more confident that classroom teachers will substantially benefit from this text. Finally, we want to express our appreciation to Doctor Byron Liggett, a neurologist, who provided helpful review criticism of the section regarding brain dysfunctions in children. His extensive experience with the treatment of this anomaly provides assurance that our information is relevant.

Contents

INFORMAL DIAGNOSTIC
ASSESSMENT
OF CHILDREN

Chapter 1

Classroom Evaluation

Chapter Objectives

- *The differing views of teachers and mental health professionals with regard to diagnostic symptoms of emotional disturbance.*
- *The problems created by identifying children by means of nonspecific and vague behavioral terms.*
- *Four variables that the teacher should consider in order to gain a realistic perspective of classroom difficulties.*
- *The assessment of verbal expressive ability.*
- *The definitions of and the difference between conduct disorders and personality disorders.*
- *The reason why teachers view conduct disorders as more important indicators of emotional disturbance than personality disorders.*
- *Variables that should be considered in the informal assessment of classroom academic abilities.*
- *The differentiation between learning disabilities caused by a central nervous system dysfunction and from psychological disorders.*
- *The reason why conduct-disordered children exhibit greater emotional problems as adults than do personality-disordered children.*
- *Statements a child may make which suggest that s/he is experiencing inadequate self-esteem regarding classroom behavior.*

THE CLASSROOM CONTINUES to be the best laboratory for identifying problems of children. Teachers and school mental health specialists must appreciate each other's positions for the potential contributions that each can make to a mutual and more comprehensive understanding of the child. Historically, these two groups of professionals have operated independently and have even resisted each other's efforts. Studies have demonstrated that teachers view overt conduct disorders as more serious indicators of emotional disturbance while mental health special-

3

ists view inner personality disorders as being the more severe (Walsh and O'Conner, 1968; Fremont et al., 1976). The criteria which are used by these two groups to arrive at these conclusions could be shared in an effort to strengthen the evaluation of children. The informal checklists at the close of this chapter are designed to be utilized for describing problems evident in the classroom. Working together or operating independently, the teacher and school diagnostician can complete these checklists as the initial phase in the informal assessment of a youngster.

Once completed, the information from the checklists should be considered in the context of each of the following chapters. Initial classroom descriptions of a child's difficulties should be viewed from developmental, neurological, and emotional viewpoints, which are presented in subsequent chapters.

The objective of this section is twofold. First, it is designed to help the teacher assess and evaluate a child's learning problems in the classroom. It is also intended to familiarize the teacher with guidelines and variables for identifying conduct and personality problems as exhibited in the school environment. Assessment is undertaken by examining such variables as academic ability, achievement motivation, perceptual functioning, and specific subject deficiencies, e.g. reading, writing, spelling, and arithmetic. In many instances of a child with learning and conduct problems, the teacher is the first to call these difficulties to attention. Upon recognizing these problems, the teacher must be able to describe them accurately and concisely. From the research on behavior modification and the recent upsurge of interest in behavioral objectives, there are now precise terms and criteria that can be used to describe a child's behavioral and learning deviations.

It is not unusual for some teachers and parents to complain about nonspecific behavior features that are described in vague and general terms: "Johnny is disruptive," "Debra has been disorderly for the past two weeks," "Jackie is irresponsible," "Alan is inattentive," "Tony is emotionally disturbed." Such comments are only meaningful to the person who related them and are of little help in identifying the problem. In order to gain a realistic perspective of learning, conduct, and personality difficulties, the teacher must keep the following four variables in mind: (1) What, specifically, are the difficulties? (2) How often do they occur? (3) What stimuli or environmental situations contribute to their occurrence? and (4) How is the problem excessive compared with other children of the same chronological age and grade level?

By describing the child's behavior in objective, observable terminology, there will be little confusion or guesswork as to the exact nature of the problem. When assessing the frequency or rate of occurrence, the relative seriousness of the problem (compared to other children) will become apparent, and it will provide baselines by which to make comparisons once remediation intervention techniques are implemented. By delineating the specific environmental situations which are associated with the occurrence of the behavioral deviation, a more comprehensive and thorough assessment of the child will result.

For appropriate diagnosis of classroom difficulties, it is sometimes helpful to investigate previous school-related problems and to gain a historical perspective about the child. Most parents are able to provide a fairly distinguishable account of a child's school experience from preschool, nursery school, or kindergarten up to the present time. This account should include adjustment to each grade level, marks earned, and attitude about school and classroom. Parents should also be encouraged to remember comments made by teachers in parent-teacher conferences which might include quasi-diagnostic descriptions of learning problems or accounts of conduct and adjustment difficulties. Any sharp change in grades should also be described. It is not uncommon for a mother to illustrate sudden changes in grades or behavior due to a divorce, a death in the family, or some other emotional upheaval. In other cases, a traumatic experience or change in residence might affect grades and behavior. If personality conflicts between a child and the teachers have occurred, this also warrants attention. Parents seem to have an uncanny knack for remembering that certain school years passed uneventfully with very productive behavior and are able to contrast those with problem-ridden years marked by pugilism, defiance, hostility, and adjustment difficulty. On still other occasions, parents might describe withdrawal or disruptive adjustment problems associated with major changes in a child's life.

The teacher should exact a detailed account of the child's present academic situation. From this description, insights into emotional disturbances and social maladjustments can be gained. Grades should be described in relation to the home situation and interpersonal classroom factors. Teachers should note any remarks made by the parents, counselors, or administrators which bear directly on the child's learning problems.

What do the school records report on intelligence and achievement test scores? What specific academic and curriculum problem is the teacher aware of? What are the child's comprehension and concentration skills? What is the quality of handwriting? How does the child follow directions? What about the quality of the child's performance and the ability to complete work? Does the child find it difficult to persist at a task, and with what kinds of tasks?

If the child has a subject of special interest, as sometimes is the case of youngsters interested in spiders and insects, then interest can be noted in the classroom. Whether the child works at, above, or below his ability level should be estimated. It is also useful to know that a child's readiness is sometimes delayed by comparison to others of the same chronological age. It is certainly not uncommon for a kindergarten youngster to remain behind classmates on prereading skills and to catch them quickly once readiness is reached.

For some cases, the teacher should ask parents to describe the domestic atmosphere regarding homework and the extent to which the family encourages or undermines those efforts. While it is sometimes common for parents to be disinterested in a child's academic achievement, it is also rather common for a parent to apply pressure for academic acceleration beyond the child's ability to produce. Either of these extremes is important and will almost certainly be reflected in the child's attitude toward school and subsequent academic performance.

LEARNING PROBLEMS

To informally assess a child's learning, the teacher should investigate the following six variables: verbal expressive abilities, curiosity-exploratory behaviors, memory and fund of knowledge, concentration, specific learning problems, and achievement levels.

Verbal Expressive Abilities

Verbal expressive ability in children is their capacity to tell what they know, describe what they perceive, and communicate how they feel. In assessing children's verbal expressive abilities, teachers can observe the following: How does the child describe being upset? How does the child resolve problems with peers when in disagreement? How does the child express abstract notions about life? And, how does s/he describe ambitions for the future? From parent-teacher conferences, what can the parent recall about previous teacher comments relative to the child's ability to use verbal expression? These criteria will be very useful in monitoring the child's verbal learning ability.

By examining verbal expressive abilities, psychologists are able to gain an understanding about the child's reasoning abilities. Children who are able to think in an abstract and divergent fashion are said to be creative. Divergent expression, one major thinking process, centers around generating a number of possible solutions to a problem or question that is raised. For example, the child might be asked "What are examples of ways to use a pen, piece of paper, stopwatch, glass bottle, and magnifying glass?" Children who are more sophisticated in their abstract and divergent thinking processes can readily cite many creative examples. Additionally, the child may be shown a picture of a face and asked to cite any words which would describe the facial expressions of the character pictured. Essentially, this approach has the child describe the various perceptions that s/he has of the picture. Another question might be, "How many ways can you use this stone?" Children with limited abstract and divergent thinking processes will reflect an impoverished pattern of response to these open-ended inquiries.

There is a second major type of thought process called convergent thinking. Convergent thinking involves the ability to apply accumulated knowledge that is needed to correctly answer a single response question. A particular thought process is necessary, and the child is expected to make one response to a rather specific question. The question might be, "When was Abraham Lincoln born?" or "What is the name of our mayor?" Convergent thinking ability is usually measured by most IQ instruments, teacher-designed tests, and achievement instruments.

Examining verbal expressive abilities gives an observer the opportunity to evaluate cognitive flow and thought flexibility and to assess the child's ability to encode information. In the event that a child experiences substantial problems in expressing cognitive material, an educational evaluation may be in order. Lack of verbal expressiveness might result from intellectual deficits, psychological conflicts, or simply from disadvantaged or limited prior experiences.

Curiosity-Exploratory Behaviors

Curiosity-exploratory behavior is the child's physical, emotional, and intellectual self-involvement with the world around him. It is the exploration of one's capacities and the finding of one's own pace and rhythm. The more self-initiated curiosity and exploratory behavior a child experiences, the greater becomes his or her ability to effectively learn in new situations.

The teacher can question the parent about a boy's familiarity with the world around him, his ability to perform with his hands, his understanding of mechanical manipulations, his aesthetic appreciation, his concerns of a religious nature, his use of books as reference sources, and his family heritage. The boy who is curious and exploratory in his behavior is likely to want to know how mechanical objects work, to ask questions about life and death, and to be dissatisfied with inadequate responses which fail to answer his questions. While all children of every age display some curiosity-exploratory behaviors, children with almost endless questions who are given reasonable direction are clearly set apart from their peers. Such curiosity drives are often associated with higher-than-average intelligence. It can be useful for the teacher to describe a child's curiosity-exploratory behavior in terms of construction projects, membership in various clubs or organizations, and experience with certain items of interest.

Memory and Fund of Knowledge

Memory is the ability to retain impressions and traces of information obtained through the visual, auditory, and other sensory modalities. Fund of knowledge is the child's reservoir of information; it is an integral part of memory. Memory is also taken as an indirect measure of a child's intellectual ability. It is important to assess such memory abilities as recent and distant memory, visual and auditory recall, and a child's ability to provide a personal historical account. In the case of memory assessment, the information must come directly from the child.

In assessing recent memory, it is sometimes useful to ask questions about a child's ability to remember what clothing was worn and what was eaten for breakfast the previous day.

In this regard, it is also useful to ask about the child's orientation in time and the ability to maintain accurate cognitive maps of the environment with which there is familiarity (orientation in space). Any attempt to retrieve information which the child has recently learned will serve to monitor recent recall. In reference to distant memory, the child can be asked to describe former teachers and classmates of earlier years. The recall of any number of earlier experiences can serve to tap distant memory.

It is of interest to note a child's description of the earliest memory. Recollections prior to two years of age usually identify precocious children. By contrast, the child who is able to remember experiences only subsequent to age six has a somewhat impoverished distant recall. In assessing both recent and distant memory, the teacher should ascertain the child's ability to describe personal history. The child may be asked about the recall of earlier childhood, complete with experiences, friends, and special events. Children are particularly interested in describing special pets they have had throughout the years and the eventual end of each of these animals. In the assessment of memory, the teacher should observe all those events which are given to the child auditorily or visually, whether academic or social, and make comparisons with other children regarding the child's ability to recall the information. Other informal methods which demand memory recall can be devised by the classroom teacher to assess memory. The more inconspicuous and informal techniques provide more reliable evaluative data about a child's memory.

Whether assessing long-term or recent memory, both the visual and auditory memory channels must be monitored. Requesting the child to retrieve information which was previously viewed will usually serve to monitor visual memory. Asking the child to describe a story, picture, playground activity, or object will aid in this process. In assessing auditory memory, the teacher is attempting to monitor the retrieval of information which was previously given through the auditory channel. The child can be asked to recall animals, first names, shapes, numbers, and voices from auditory memory. Assessing the child's performance for learning via the visual or auditory channels will give the teacher additional insights into the child's learning abilities. Some children can be described as visual learners and others as auditory learners, while some have no major preference for a sensory modality. Some children have been found to learn by only one sensory channel and purposely avoid other sensory input while attempting to learn. For instance, a youngster may not maintain eye contact while the teacher is talking in order to understand the information given auditorily. Encouraging eye contact with simultaneous auditory messages may result in confusing the information offered. The teacher must take these variables into consideration when assessing the visual and auditory memory channels.

Concentration

An assessment of children's ability to concentrate will provide an estimate of their capacity to maintain attention and adhere to classroom requirements. Children who cannot attend to a matter for more than a few minutes are likely to be described as distractible and impulsive. The lack of ability to concentrate and maintain a reasonable attention span will provide some insights into learning problems. Although there are no agreed-upon standards as to how long a child should be able to concentrate or attend to a particular task, the teacher can assess such abilities by comparing a particular child with classmates. The teacher should develop an awareness of the child who consistently manifests inattentiveness as contrasted to the child who attends well but only to a few topics of interest. Moreover, the teacher must be alert to the child who shows large discrepancies in attentiveness on a daily or periodic basis.

In assessment of attention span and memory, it is inappropriate to describe children simply by saying that they have a "short attention span" or are "inattentive." Both of these abilities usually involve the visual and auditory sensory modalities. Thus, to speak in terms of visual inattentiveness, auditory inattentiveness, visual memory deficits, and auditory memory deficits, regardless of the combination, provides a more exact and precise description of a child's learning abilities. For example, a fourth-grade child regularly forgot oral instruction after a short length of time. This reflects either auditory inattentiveness or auditory memory deficit and should be diagnosed further. Another child appears to disregard written directions for homework assignments and repeatedly asks for help to decipher written instructions on the chalkboard. These are symptoms of visual inattentiveness or visual memory deficits.

Once these variables have been taken into account, the teacher will begin to understand the child's academic history. Memory impairments, concentration deficits, and poor expressive abilities will parallel learning problems. In conversing with a child, the teacher will note the extent and depth of the youngster's knowledge in those areas that represent a special interest to him. By investigating the fund of knowledge, observers gain more insights into a child's intellectual functioning.

Specific Learning Problems

Educators are becoming increasingly aware of differences in learning abilities of elementary students. Some students who have average to above-average intelligence are not able to achieve at grade level in various academic subjects. A specific learning problem is the inability of this type of child to perform adequately in one or more of the major academic areas, i.e. reading, arithmetic, or spelling. In many cases, children identified as having a specific learning disability will also have associated psychological problems.

Common learning disabilities are thought to be caused from central nervous system dysfunctions. Because of a nervous system "dysfunction," learning becomes impaired. These children, consequently, must learn by special education methods. According to Ross (1967), classical learning difficulties could arise from two factors, central nervous system dysfunctions or psychological trauma. Although psychologically caused learning difficulties are not commonly understood or recognized by educators, they should be identified when possible.

In the event the learning difficulties arise from a central nervous system dysfunction, the remediation is basically educational. Should the difficulty arise from characteristic emotional dynamics, the remediation is psychological. In most cases of learning disabilities, the remediation is educational for correcting perception-related handicaps. However, in some instances, treatment of perceptual handicaps may be ineffective because it concentrates on educational factors and does not take into account the accompanying psychological symptoms. In any case, a thorough evaluation of causal factors will consider both educational and psychological symptoms. For example, a child who experiences a trauma at home may display subsequent educational deficits. A child who is shouted at while reading may display subsequent reading deficits. The child who has experienced repeated failure in math exercises at the chalkboard is a prime candidate for abusive behavior of a psychological nature on the playground. Such difficulties are examples of the relationship between psychological and educational symptoms of learning problems. Both instances demand psychological intervention. It is best before referring a child for learning disorder evaluation to include any data which might be suggestive of the causal factors producing the learning difficulties. Such information will encourage and facilitate a more comprehensive assessment of the child's learning difficulties and accurately identify remediation. A more detailed discussion of the central nervous system learning difficulties is found in Chapter 3.

Achievement Levels

Learning assessment of the child in the classroom should include careful analysis of specific subject deficiencies. Deficiencies are usually defined in terms of expected achievement grade level minus actual achievement grade level or the distance, in months and years, that the child is behind average peers in the same grade. The teacher can determine the need for formalized educational testing by informally determining deficiencies and investigating performance in other academic areas. Having identified subject deficiencies, the teacher may then refer the child for formalized testing procedures to identify the causal factors producing the problems. If, for example, perceptual problems are found, based on the test results, a remediation program should be designed and implemented. If formalized testing does not reveal perceptual dysfunctions, the teacher should explore the child's interest in deficient subject matter in more detail as well as thoroughly investigate any emotional rationale for inadequate performance. However, it would not be unusual to find that a child was performing poorly due to lack of interest in the subject matter. If, on the other hand, the intellectual assessment parallels classroom productivity, a youngster is probably working at expected capacity. A comparison of intellectual abilities with school performance provides good diagnostic indicators and contributes to a system of checks and balances. The record may indicate capabilities, or it may reveal discrepancies between a child's ability and performance levels. This information is diagnostic in nature and is readily assessable through the descriptions of the child in the classroom atmosphere. The diagnosis of underachievement is identifiable through the comparison of intelligence and current academic achievement. The academic diagnostic levels of achievement are underachievement, expected achievement, or overachievement. Underachievement is most common, while expected achievement is fairly common and overachievement is quite rare.

CASE STUDY I

Teacher's Report (Janet F., 9 years old, 4th grade)

Janet was referred for an evaluation by her teacher because she has been displaying a number of behavioral and academic problems in the school setting. Other children tease, mimic, and annoy her. Janet elicits this behavior in her peers by excessive talking, tattling, and telling wild tales. She has shown consistent academic failure in most subjects and, according to the Iowa Basic Skills Test given in September, Janet achieved second grade level in the core academic areas, except in arithmetic where she scored on a sixth grade level.

Janet is characterized by carelessness, failing grades, handwriting illegibility, specific deficiencies in reading and spelling, and moderate deficits in visual and auditory memory. She usually forgets her pencils, books, or other articles and consistently asks to borrow from peers. Her written work is not legible and, as a result, she cannot perform on assignments which demand writing. Even when asked to spell orally, she typically misses most of the words. Carelessness is manifested by losing objects, spilling paint on her clothes, and dropping books off her desk. It is difficult to take a baseline because this activity occurs all of the time. She has difficulty recalling auditory instructions and cannot repeat the main theme of a story. Problems in the conduct area are indicated in terms of Janet's constant interrupting of others, impulsivity, tattling, and giving up easily on academic tasks in the face of difficulty. Personality problems manifest themselves in excessive crying, anxiety, withdrawal, unhappiness, and lack of acceptance by the peer groups.

Alternative Solutions

1. Obtain more specific information about her problem.
2. Recommend a formal psychological and educational evaluation.
3. Place her in a class for emotionally disturbed children.
4. Recommend counseling for her acting out behavior.

Recommended Solution (Janet F., 9 years old, 4th grade)

Some very specific behavioral problems as well as academic deficits were given in the reason for referral. Thus, to have opted for alternative 1 would have been superfluous, as this information is given. Janet is suffering from obvious social difficulties. These are shown by her excessive talking, tattling, telling stories, and by the other children teasing and mimicking her. Moreover, she has specific problems of attention span, handwriting legibility, reading, spelling, visual and auditory memory, and general disorganization. From these symptoms, a psychological and educational evaluation should be given, as indicated in alternative 2. To place her in a class for emotionally disturbed children would have only served to overlook many of the problems that she is presently experiencing and provide treatment before the exact disorder is defined. Thus, at this point, option 3 is not a suitable alternative. This child needs to be evaluated so that recommendations and prescriptions for her social and educational deficits can be initiated. Option 2 is the best alternative. To have recommended option 4, counseling only, neglects some very important diagnostic symptoms concerning educational deficits. Thus, it is as reasonable to assume that her learning problems may have caused her emotional problems as it is to say that the emotional problems caused her learning problems. Therefore, to recommend counseling for the behavior problems would only serve to monitor part of the problem. In some cases, counseling may be sufficient to enable the child to function better in both the academic and psychological areas. In such cases, the prior problems would have been primarily psychological in nature. Furthermore, an educational program may produce similar results, i.e. an improved academic and psychological status. Consequently a dual approach using both psychological and educational assessment devices will lead to a more thorough and sophisticated evaluation.

CLASSROOM BEHAVIOR PROBLEMS

This section concentrates on the child's behavioral and emotional characteristics as they relate to the classroom atmosphere. The very early and accurate diagnosis of emotional disturbance in children is a challenge toward which members of mental health professions direct a great deal of energy. Studies about the differences in perceptions of emotional disturbance in children have indicated that classroom teachers do not agree with mental health specialists. Wickman (1928), one of the first to analyze ratings of childhood problems which predict emotional disturbance, reported that teachers viewed overt behavioral problems as the more salient indicators of emotional disturbance. Clinical psychologists, psychiatrists, and psychiatric social workers were reported to perceive intrapsychic emotional difficulties (within the individual) as more severe and lasting symptoms. Beilin (1959), in a review of forty-seven related research articles, confirmed the finding submitted by Wickman.

In 1968, Walsh and O'Connor used psychiatrists, psychologists (mental health specialists), and teachers in a study designed to differentiate how these professionals classified indicators of emotional disturbance. The mental health specialists indicated that such variables as soiling, wetting, exposing oneself, sadness, and peculiar ideas were the more prominent symptoms. Teachers ranked hurting others, defiance, temper tantrums, and excessive fighting as the more likely symptoms. Here again, teachers were ranking overt behavioral problems as the more important indicators, while the mental health specialists listed intrapsychic disorders as the more significant indicators of emotional disturbance.

While studying the reported behavior problems of elementary school children, Peterson (1961) used two persistent classifications of problem characteristics. He labeled these categories as *conduct* and *personality* disorders. Using a sample of 831 elementary school children, Peterson found distinct differences in their behavioral attributes. The conduct-disordered youngster was defined as a child who made others the victim of his/her behavior and was characterized as disobedient, disruptive, destructive, boisterous, etc. S/he is typically identified as being antisocial. Personality-disordered children were characterized as anxious, depressed, aloof, tense, and were identified as children experiencing inner personality disorders where the child himself was made victim of his/her own conflicts. Additionally, antisocial or conduct-disordered children demonstrate greater emotional problems as adults compared to those who exhibit personality disorders (Robins, 1966). In view of the research on conduct disorders and the emphasis which mental health professionals place on personality disorders, both variables should be considered with equal seriousness as diagnostic indicators of emotional disturbance. Conduct and personality characteristics are detailed in the checklists at the end of the chapter. Some of the most obvious and subtle behavior difficulties are given so as to provide the teacher with latitude in identifying classroom behavior deviations.

The conduct disorder category consists of those activities which interfere with the behavior of other individuals and society. The personality disorder category is composed of those items which reflect intrapsychic features, with the child being the victim of these psychological conflicts. Conduct-disordered children exhibit behavior which is negative to others because it affects them directly. Some of them are characterized as being aggressive toward individuals and society with such behavior as defiance, belligerence, and bullying. Personality-disordered children may or may not exhibit problem behavior. If problem behavior is exhibited, it becomes obvious that the conflict is within the child, such as with depression, nervousness, and stuttering. Furthermore, this child does not aggress on society in contrast to the child with a conduct disorder. Another difference is that personality disorders are more difficult to recognize while conduct disorders, by their very nature, must be affecting others in order to be identified as such. There are also a number of children who exhibit a combination of behaviors which resists exclusive identification in either the conduct or personality categories; such youngsters may be described appropriately in both checklists. The following discussion of personality and conduct disorders in the classroom makes no attempt to treat them separately or independently of each other. The discussion does not attempt to cover all the behavior problems found in the classroom but only those considered serious by mental health specialists. However, the checklists at the end of the chapter are separated into specific disorders for clarity of questioning, accurate identification, and for referral to specialists. This section will provide the teacher with salient and identifiable variables of conduct and personality behaviors exhibited in the classroom. While the literature is replete with studies, lists, and instruments for rating a child's behavior (Spivack and Swift, 1967; Spivack, Haimes, Spotts, 1967; Burks, 1968; Myklebust, 1971; and Conners, 1969), the emphasis here is on the comprehensive list of the most salient variables for informal assessment of classroom difficulties.

CASE STUDY II

Teacher's Report (Ted W., 11 years old, 6th grade)

Barely eleven years old, Ted is the youngest sixth-grade student in Mr. Davison's homeroom class. The sixth grade is semidepartmentalized, and Ted has two other teachers along with Mr. Davison; each teacher is responsible for two hours of contact during the school day. Mr. Davison is Ted's only male teacher and seems to be the only teacher who has significant trouble in getting Ted interested in learning.

Ted is the only child of parents who are in their middle forties. Ted's father is frequently away from home with his work but seems to be intensely interested in establishing a positive relationship with Ted. In conferences with the family, Ted seems rather indifferent to his father and very attentive to his mother, much like his behavior with Mr. Davison and the two female teachers who work with Ted in school.

In Mr. Davison's class, Ted daydreams excessively, expresses behavior bordering on temper tantrums when reprimanded to do his work, sulks for long periods of time, defies other students' efforts to help him, and openly criticizes peers' good academic work. Specifically, he stares at his reading material for fifteen to twenty minutes three or four times during the school day, and, on eight occasions, he attempted to hit Mr. Davison when he grabbed Ted by the arms in effort to remind him to complete his work. Further, he openly teased two female students when they had completed their assignments. He will not let other children help him and has been known to fight with them and shout that he does not need their assistance. One day, he pushed down three peers while on the playground and challenged them to a fight. These were the same children who earlier offered to help him with his assignments. He is often belligerent about following instructions or taking criticism, usually blaming a class neighbor for his own faults. All of his disruptive, negative behavior is restricted to Mr. Davison's class, and he is reported as a model student in the other classes.

Alternative Solutions

1. Use negative reinforcement to extinguish such behaviors as day-dreaming, tantrums, and criticism of his peers. On the other hand, use positive reinforcement to augment attention span and facilitate adjustment in the above mentioned areas.
2. Since all of the behaviors occur in Mr. Davison's class, remove Ted and place him in another class with a female teacher.
3. Investigate more specifically the variables which are associated antecedently with Ted's behavioral disorders.
4. Refer the child to the principal for appropriate discipline.

Recommended Solution (Ted W., 11 years old, 6th grade)

Although option 1 may serve to reduce Ted's inappropriate behavior and facilitate better adjustment, it does not supply information as to the contributing factors concerning his disorder. Specifically, there is no information as to those variables which contribute to the child's inappropriate behavior. It is of interest to note that of the three instructors, Ted has problems with only the one male teacher. Since the one male teacher is the primary variable which has changed in Ted's environment it might, in fact, be the contributing factor to Ted's inappropriate behavior. Based on the above, option 2 would not give any information as to the specific contributing factors concerning Ted's inappropriate behavior. To place Ted in another sixth grade class would not alleviate the basic problem which is still existent within his own psychological structure. Option 3 is the most appropriate, since it addresses investigating those variables which precede Ted's inappropriate behavioral patterns. Thus, by ascertaining the contributing factors such as the teacher's attitude and the attitude of other students toward Ted, as well as the way academic assignments are presented to him, a great deal of information may be obtained concerning Ted's reaction to these variables. It might be that a minimal change by Mr. Davison in the class structure, curriculum, and other aspects of the classroom environment would be sufficient to produce changes in Ted's attitude. On the other hand, it might be that once these contributing variables are identified and minimal changes in the environment do not effect behavioral changes, the school psychologist or counselor should become involved. It would be inappropriate to opt for alternative 4 as discipline does not facilitate better adjustment to the learning environment. It may, in fact, encourage Ted not to display the inappropriate behaviors, but the major conflicts would still be within his response repertoire. In other situations, Ted may still display the maladaptive behavior. Thus, discipline may have a short-term effect in reducing the inappropriate behaviors, but over the long term, it can only be detrimental to the child.

Identification of Conduct and Personality Deviations in the Classroom

Children who worry excessively or who tend to flee into their worlds of private things and thoughts will suggest a type of pathology worthy of investigation. Such an emotional disorder may be characterized by excessive withdrawal from the peer group and physical detachment from objects and people. The child who is preoccupied, nervous, and tense may also reveal psychopathology. Children who display other psychological problems such as nailbiting, enuresis, stuttering, and isolation should also be targets of concern and are all examples of personality deviations.

Excessive tattling, hair pulling, attention seeking, and cruelty are examples of conduct disorders that are readily identified by teachers. On a social level, a child's attitude toward school may be revealed by his previous record. The youngster who fights excessively with peers is probably struggling for some sort of recognition or survival from others by whom s/he feels victimized. Excessive demands of teacher's attention, incessant talking, and social interaction difficulties are telltale danger signs. The child who has no friends, who tends to reject others and be rejected by them, may be displaying behavior designed to avoid interpersonal closeness and threat of emotional hurt. In such a case, it may be more comfortable to deny oneself the privilege of friendship than to risk the possibility of failure in a relationship.

It is important to be alert to social or cultural differences about which the child may or may not feel sensitive. While nearly all children come to school reasonably well dressed and in reasonably good health, there are exceptions in which families are destitute and without appropriate nutrition and clothing. Carefully selected questions will invite a child to describe the family's struggle for survival and possibly provide insights into the social and cultural deficiencies which may have stimulated inappropriate behavior or sensitivity to the opinions of others. A child who comes to school with hand-me-down and patched clothing may feel inadequate next to children with an attractive school wardrobe. Financial status of a family is therefore important if it significantly affects a child's behavior and appearance in the classroom.

Still other children are affected by what they perceive to be competition with the teacher's pet, especially if it inadvertently removes them from previously favored status with a teacher. One first-grade girl felt herself in high favor with her teacher, for whom she produced diligently. In the middle of the school year, another child transferred into the classroom, captured this child's favored position, and went on to earn generous attention and interaction with the teacher. At that point, the first child dropped her level of productivity, became disillusioned with her teacher, and suffered a traumatic experience in losing a certain social status in that classroom.

Other children have learned to escape unpleasant classroom activities by developing physical or somatic complaints such as stomachaches, headaches, and vomiting. Or, they may make use of less specific symptoms and state, "I don't feel well," suggesting that they are experiencing a systemic physical disorder. Another child may become easily upset and overreact to minimal stimuli such as being angered at the breaking of a pencil point or crying if a correct answer cannot be supplied at the request by the teacher. Persistent personality symptoms such as these suggest the child is in need of psychological evaluation.

Rapid and alternating mood changes are indicative of personality problems and may be exemplified by the child moving from euphoria to sadness within a few minutes or periodically during the school day. Inadequate self-esteem characterizes the child who constantly states an inability to accomplish routine classroom tasks and who refuses to indulge in new adventures, thus preventing the experience of new situations because of fear of failure. The teacher can identify those children by noting comments that have a self-depreciating tone. The child may have been heard to say, "I can't do anything right," "I'm not good enough," "I always lose when I play," or "I wish I were dead." Such children are anxious, lack self-confidence, and are highly indecisive. It is always important to be alert to the child who withdraws or daydreams and becomes intensely involved with internal ideations that prevent attending to routine responsibilities. These are serious personality problems that need attention.

Excessive anxiety attached to specific situations such as participation in competitive sports, taking a test, and talking in a group discussion may also indicate emotional stress. Examples are the child who is hesitant and anxious about taking spelling tests or one who exhibits unusual anxiety while participating in softball. Some children may experience stuttering associated with heightened anxiety as well as other articulation problems. Body tics, excessive mouthing, and biting may also be anxiety based. Although these problems may seem minimal, they should be seriously investigated, with the possibility of referral for a psychological evaluation. It is important to be aware that behavior problems sometimes suggest that the child is suffering from an internal conflict or more deeply rooted problem. The external or obvious behavior that is readily noticed when children transgress on themselves or others may result from an unobvious psychological disorder.

Such symptoms as depression, hallucinations, and excessive fantasy are sometimes difficult to identify and can be confused with disorders of attention. Lack of interest and inattentiveness are often indicators of more deeply rooted problems such as the ones stated above. One child was known to experience auditory hallucinations, but he appeared to the school psychologist to be inattentive. Applying behavior modification techniques only served to remove an important diagnostic symptom of a deeply disturbed youngster. The techniques were successful in lengthening the child's attention span. Months later, the child was questioned about the experiences he was having when he was inattentive and it was recognized that he was suffering from auditory hallucinations centering around the death of a relative. The major symptoms were hallucinations, but the child demonstrated what appeared to be inattentiveness. Although no attempt is made to train the reader to diagnose problems which are deep seated and not readily apparent, it is important to be aware that behavioral deviations occasionally reflect emotional conflict.

As indicated earlier, research suggests that teachers are more concerned with conduct-disordered than with personality-disordered youngsters and that mental health specialists view the situation conversely. Consequently, it behooves both professions to take each type of disorder seriously, especially when it hinders a child's healthy adjustment to his home, his peers, and his learning.

The following are the checklists designed to informally assess learning, conduct, and personality problems, respectively. (This text views children with conduct problems as victimizing others and those with personality problems as victimizing themselves.) The checklists are prepared for use by the teacher and school mental health specialist, or by both as a mutual effort. Any checklist item is scored on an intensity dimension from none to excessive. These checklists will assist in describing classroom problems in specific terms and will serve to stimulate accurate identification of difficulties. Comparisons can then be made to other class peers for diagnostic determination. When comparing, it may be discovered that many of the pupils are described in the same excessive terms attributed to the child in question. In this case, it becomes the responsibility of the school mental health specialist to assist the teacher and/or to independently make accurate diagnostic impressions. In still other instances, the teacher will discover that the target child is not displaying excessive difficulty and that further assessment is unnecessary. The problem can be handled by making minor changes in the classroom structure. When the use of these checklists clearly identifies excessive problems by comparison to other children, the teacher may proceed with planning, further informal assessment as described in succeeding chapters, or formal psychological testing for an in-depth diagnostic workup.

Learning Problems	*None*	*Mild*	*Intensity* *Moderate*	*Excessive*
Lack of interest and curiosity	___	___	___	___
Failure to finish work	___	___	___	___
Inability to follow directions	___	___	___	___
Achievement anxiety	___	___	___	___
Short attention span	___	___	___	___
Carelessness	___	___	___	___
Poor comprehension	___	___	___	___
Impoverished fund of knowledge	___	___	___	___
Distractibility	___	___	___	___
Lack of integration of senses	___	___	___	___
Motor incoordination fine	___	___	___	___
gross	___	___	___	___
Dullness, slowness	___	___	___	___
Impaired concentration	___	___	___	___
Failing grades	___	___	___	___
Handwriting errors	___	___	___	___
Speech deficiency	___	___	___	___
Mathematics deficiency	___	___	___	___
Reading deficiency	___	___	___	___
Spelling deficiency	___	___	___	___
Memory deficit visual long-term	___	___	___	___
recent	___	___	___	___

auditory
   long-term   —— —— —— ——
   recent   —— —— —— ——
   rote   —— —— —— ——
Disorganization   —— —— —— ——
Sloppiness   —— —— —— ——
Inability to think abstractly   —— —— —— ——
Inability to attack new
   learning   —— —— —— ——
Inability to plan ahead   —— —— —— ——
Perseveration
   motor   —— —— —— ——
   verbal   —— —— —— ——
Vocabulary limitations   —— —— —— ——
Lack of motivation   —— —— —— ——
Miscellaneous

————————   —— —— —— ——

————————   —— —— —— ——

————————   —— —— —— ——

Conduct Problems
Abusive language
Accusing   —— —— —— ——
Annoying and teasing   —— —— —— ——
Attention seeking   —— —— —— ——
Belligerent   —— —— —— ——
Fault finding   —— —— —— ——
   with others
   with self   —— —— —— ——
Bossy, bullying tactics   —— —— —— ——
Cheating, underhandedness   —— —— —— ——
Clinging   —— —— —— ——
Competitiveness   —— —— —— ——
Complaining   —— —— —— ——

	None	Mild	Intensity Moderate	Excessive
Disruptiveness	_____	_____	_____	_____
Cruelty				
to animals	_____	_____	_____	_____
to children	_____	_____	_____	_____
Defiance	_____	_____	_____	_____
Destructiveness	_____	_____	_____	_____
Disrespect	_____	_____	_____	_____
Excitability	_____	_____	_____	_____
Unfriendliness	_____	_____	_____	_____
Impulsiveness	_____	_____	_____	_____
Interrupting	_____	_____	_____	_____
Lying	_____	_____	_____	_____
Overactiveness	_____	_____	_____	_____
Improper out-of-seat behavior	_____	_____	_____	_____
Pugilism (hitting, fighting)	_____	_____	_____	_____
Defeatism	_____	_____	_____	_____
Lack of sense of fair play	_____	_____	_____	_____
Inclination to play with smaller children	_____	_____	_____	_____
Rejection by peers	_____	_____	_____	_____
Telling of wild stories	_____	_____	_____	_____
Reliance upon others	_____	_____	_____	_____
Resentment toward criticism	_____	_____	_____	_____
Resistance to discipline	_____	_____	_____	_____
Stealing	_____	_____	_____	_____
Stubbornness	_____	_____	_____	_____
Throwing of tantrums	_____	_____	_____	_____
Tattling	_____	_____	_____	_____

Truancy

Vengefulness

Miscellaneous

_____

_____

_____

Personality Problems

Apathy

Avoidance of others

Body rocking

Mood changes

Tendency to cry easily

Daydreaming, fantasizing

Defeatist attitude

Delusions

Depression

Flight of ideas

Guilt (remorse)

Guiltlessness (no remorse)

Hair twisting or pulling

Hallucinations

    visual

    auditory

Impatience

Inappropriateness of

    responses

Lack of reality awareness

Lack of confidence

Low frustration tolerance

Low stress tolerance

Nervousness, anxiety

Phobias, fearfulness

	None	Mild	*Intensity* Moderate	Excessive
Physical complaints				
headaches	___	___	___	___
stomachaches	___	___	___	___
other	___	___	___	___
Poor self-concept	___	___	___	___
Sensitivity	___	___	___	___
Shyness	___	___	___	___
Incontinence				
of urine	___	___	___	___
of feces	___	___	___	___
Stuttering	___	___	___	___
Talking to self	___	___	___	___
Thumb sucking	___	___	___	___
Tics	___	___	___	___
Unhappiness	___	___	___	___
Unpopularity	___	___	___	___
Withdrawing	___	___	___	___
Worrying	___	___	___	___
Miscellaneous				
_____	___	___	___	___
_____	___	___	___	___

SUGGESTED READINGS

Becker, W. C., Engelmann, S., and Thomas, D. R.: *Teaching. 1: Classroom Management.* Chicago, Science Research Associates, 1975.

This book will help clarify and give additional examples of how to describe elementary students in objective and measurable terms. It is basically a book concerned with behavior modification principles and gives numerous examples for improving teacher interactions with elementary school-age youngsters. *Class-*

room Management offers program practice exercises as well as suggestions to monitor the academic performance and behavior of children. It has several sections devoted to defining and counting behavior and offers recording sheets for obtaining baseline data. It concentrates on such areas as conduct problems, punishment, criticism, and peer involvement and specifies precise means for dealing with tantrums, fighting, hitting, cheating, and delinquent-type behaviors.

Mann, P. H., and Suiter, P.: *Handbook in Diagnostic Teaching. A Learning Disabilities Approach,* abridged ed. Boston, Allyn and Bacon, Inc., 1974.

The book by Mann and Suiter is well suited for teachers in regular education and special education classrooms. The manuscript presents developmental reading and spelling inventories. The inventories are designed to spot specific problems that children are having within particular subject areas. Common academic problems are identified along with specific emphasis on assessment of the auditory and visual channels. Diagnostic testing is presented for motor deficits, handwriting errors, and language. Attention is devoted to affective components, and in all areas where deficits are identified, educational activities are presented in a prescriptive manner. This book is highly recommended for the teacher interested in learning more about informal assessment and remediation.

Hively, W., and Reynolds, M. C. (Eds.): *Domain-Referenced Testing in Special Education.* Minneapolis, Leadership Training Institute/Special Education, University of Minnesota, 1975.

Domain-referenced testing has been more commonly referred to as criterion-referenced testing or objective-referenced testing. This approach has much in common with a teacher's informal diagnostic assessment of children. The commonality rests with the fact that both of these approaches attempt to individualize educational processes for school age individuals. *Domain-Referenced Testing in Special Education,* edited by Hively and Reynolds, is a collection of readings which attempts to specify the benefits and pitfalls of evaluating handicapped children. Similarities and differences between normed-referenced psychometric and domain-referenced testing are presented. Practical, theoretical, ethical, and social issues are introduced. Additionally, past and present concerns of the atypical child are given along with the impact of various types of testing programs. Furthermore, information is presented on perceptual skills curriculum and test construction.

Chapter 2

Developmental History

Chapter Objectives

- Expressive and receptive language development and a course of action for a child who shows gross delays in these areas.
- Definition and diagnostic indicators of tics.
- Parallel and cooperative play and the implications of excessive solitary play by the preschool child.
- The characteristics of abnormal fecal or urine retention by the preschool child.
- Movements which are excessive for a preschool or elementary school-age child.
- The developmental spiral and how it may be evident in the early developmental stages of children.
- The concept of laterality in relation to other developmental problems.
- The approximate age levels in years and months for walking, talking, and hand preference.
- The course of action that should be taken with a preschool or elementary school-age child who has not shown a differentiation of emotionality and support a rationale for the action.
- A more analytical referral for a psychological, neurological, or communicative disorder; for other specialized assessment, the information that should be included in the referral data.
- Three diagnostic indicators of child abuse and a plan of action where its occurrence is suspected.

THE DEVELOPMENTAL HISTORY is intended to provide a more thorough, holistic picture of the school-age child rather than to view the child in a segmented fashion. This chapter is de-. signed especially for the preschool as well as elementary school teacher. The developmental history section should give the teacher information for determining if the child is developing or has developed in a healthy manner. This section concentrates on the developmental milestones from birth to approximately five years of age or through early childhood. No attempt is made to investigate physical growth and weight variables, as these are best left to medical practitioners, and this information is not particularly helpful in the diagnostic assessment of learning problems.

Frequently, elementary school-age children are identified as having emotional or academic deficits without considering the causal factors or noting that these problems may have existed from earlier developmental stages. Often, developmental problems manifest themselves during the preschool years (ages 3-5); thus it is important that teachers become familiar with these variables. By studying developmental variables, the teacher can discover how children develop their present symptomatology. Attention to developmental dynamics may uncover the root cause of problems that parents have been unable to explain. Knowing early history enables the teacher to establish an informal baseline to monitor the child's developmental growth in comparison to other children of the same approximate chronological age.

By studying the developmental variables, clues may be obtained for planning effective remediation programs within the classroom. Finally, by understanding developmental norms, the teacher will establish a solid basis for determining whether a child should be referred to another specialist.

In the developmental assessment, it is the responsibility of the teacher to systematically define and describe the child's condition. The condition may be identified in terms of a behavioral and/or functional definition. A behavioral definition states in precise terms exactly what is objectively observed or lacking in the child's response to the environment. For example, one child is described as wetting clothing, another as not standing alone, and another as stuttering. These examples are incomplete in describing a child with a behavioral definition, as two variables, rate and duration, should be included. The *rate* is the number of times or frequency the target behavior occurs, and the *duration* is the length of time the target behavior occurs and does not occur. Using the behavioral definition, accompanied by rate and duration, the teacher can describe the child more accurately. Giving base rates allows further important comparisons to be made. For example, the teacher can tell over time whether the behavior is improving, worsening, or maintaining. For example, in class, Johnny falls to the floor from his desk six times (rate) during the three-hour morning session (duration). This behavior has occurred over the last three days (duration). Another child is described as staring off into space on the average of three times per hour (rate) during the afternoon sessions of the school day (duration). While it will not always be possible to use duration and frequency when giving a child a behavioral definition, this information significantly supplements a referral. A functional definition centers upon the causes or etiology of the target behavior, and it is based upon an objective behavioral definition. Examples of functional definitions are as follows. Five-year-old Tommy is inattentive because he has impaired hearing. It is suspected that Susie will not actively participate in athletic events because she has one or several problems, which may include poor hand-eye coordination, visual deficits, and/or neurological problems. Dmitriev (1974) sums up the value of a functional definition. "Frequently an accurate functional definition can be ar-

TABLE I

Child's Name, Age	Behavioral Definition (Frequency-Duration)	Functional Definition (Causation-Etiology)
John W., 4 years	Chews fingernails, erasers, and rubber bands throughout the morning session.	Anxious, worried?
David K., 3.5 years	Will not speak or utter sounds to peers or teacher during the entire school day.	Hearing impaired? Psychologically disturbed?
Sally A., 5 years	Soils pants 3 times during entire school day for the last four weeks.	Medical problem? Preoccupied with classroom activities? Developmental regression?
Leonard C., 3 years	Withdraws and talks to himself alone in the back of the room. Occurs about 6 different times per day and lasts from 5 to 15 minutes.	Emotionally disturbed? Threatened by peers? Has not learned socialization skills?

rived at only after a medical or psychological examination; nevertheless, an indication by the teacher of what he believes to be a functional basis of the disorder can be helpful in seeking further professional assistance."

In describing a child who needs referral to another specialist, it is the behavioral definition which will give the specialists sufficient data for further evaluation. However, any additional information which can be included in the functional definition will be useful. Table I gives a comparison of the two definitions.

CASE STUDY III

Teacher's Report (Christopher N., 5 years old, kindergarten)

This youngster is enjoying his first semester at Roosevelt school. During a typical morning in the kindergarten classroom Chris displays bursts of energy and exploratory and curiosity-motivated behavior about most new situations introduced in the classroom. He becomes very excitable about everything from snakes, gerbils, and ants to planned field trips and even to the addition of a new class member. He frequently questions the teacher about why she is doing things with and for the class and often volunteers to help her so that he can be involved with the activities. He displays this questioning behavior with fellow classmates and enjoys participating in group activities. Chris talks about what he is doing, usually in detail and with quite a lot of imagination. He sometimes seems almost obsessed about situations related to the police, firemen, doctors, Indians, and various other people, and he regularly plays these roles in his own colorful stories about the characters and situations. He enjoys acting as a policeman or fireman, sometimes gathering other children to participate in imaginary situations. Pretending there is a fire or "shoot out" are the basic themes of his activity centering around the police, Indians, etc. This behavior occurs one or two times during the school day and lasts for about 10 minutes. He often requests to nap with a toy gun and sometimes his Indian headgear.

Chris has a short attention span for activities that do not interest him, and he searches out things to do which tend to satisfy his momentary level of interest and curiosity. Chris is competitive with other children when he engages in a game and seems disappointed about not winning, especially if he feels that he was not treated fairly or if he thinks the game did not give him an equal opportunity to win. He gets fussy and cries when he finally tires out from his high level of activity and involvement with the kindergarten class routines.

Alternative Solutions

1. Investigate and detail the events which occur prior to his "obsessed" behavior so that insight will be gained as to the variables that contribute to this activity.
2. Alert the parents to the child's behavior and ask for their advice as to how to manage him in the classroom.
3. Request to have another teacher observe his activities and attempt to determine if the child is manifesting behavior which is uncharacteristic of that age group.
4. Do not attempt further informal or formal evaluation because the behavior is characteristic for this age group.

Recommended Solution
(Christopher N., 5 years old, kindergarten)

If there is any disturbance that can be identified from the teacher's report it centers around Christopher's "obsession" with policemen, firemen, doctors, Indians, etc. It is also reported that he "regularly plays these roles in his own colorful stories about the characters and situations." Attention span is considered short. Shortness of attention span is directly related to the interest and curiosity that Christopher has in the topic. Such behavior is not unusual for a five-year-old child. He is described as being competitive, disappointed when losing, and becoming "fussy" when tired with involvement in kindergarten class routines. Again, it is not unusual for five-year-old kindergarten children to demonstrate the above and become tired after experiencing high levels of activity.

Alternative 1 suggests to investigate and detail the events which occur prior to his "obsessed" behavior so that insight will be gained as to the variables that contribute to this activity. There may be numerous variables which could be identified that contribute to the alleged obsessed behavior. This behavior is typical of five-year-old children, and it is certainly not indicative of emotional problems. Thus, alternative 1 is not suitable. The teacher making this report should have been more careful as to the use of the term *obsessed* because generally speaking, obsessed refers to thought activity which is excessive and that which an individual cannot terminate. That is, thinking becomes centered on an event or particular subject and is not terminated voluntarily.

Alternative 2 suggests that the teacher ask advice from the parents on managing the child in the classroom. This alternative is not suitable because no definitive behavioral problems have been defined. Parents are likely to request from the teacher specifics on the problems that have been identified. If specific behavioral disorders are not identified, then management techniques cannot be implemented. Furthermore, it is unlikely that parents would be able to contribute to fostering better management techniques in the classroom, as they are not trained in this area.

Alternative 3 has many merits. It is commendable that a teacher would want to check perceptions of behavior with another teacher. It is likely that the other teacher would find that the behavior is not "obsessive" or atypical for children of this age. However, if the second teacher did find that the behavior was atypical, then the child should be referred for a more in-depth evaluation by a mental health professional. In this case, according to the teacher's report, there is nothing to suggest that the child is experiencing problems which would necessitate referral.

Alternative 4 is a preferable alternative. No definitive psychological, educational, or learning problems have been identified, and this. behavior is fairly typical for children of this age group.

For a comprehensive developmental investigation up to age five, the teacher needs to study three major areas: (1) neurological development, (2) affective development, and (3) social development. In each of these three sections, both normal and maladaptive developmental variables are discussed. When possible, developmental norms are provided.

NEUROLOGICAL DEVELOPMENT

An assessment of physical and neurological development up to age five is useful in identifying behavioral deviations. In studying the neurological development of the child, it is important to include such variables as motor activity, trauma, medical and sensory complications, seizure disorders, receptive and expressive language, and elimination patterns.

As opportunities are presented, the teacher should make observations concerning the general physical appearance of the child. Mannerisms and excessive movements which are beyond the ordinary can be noted. Frequent movements of the head, tongue (lip licking), arms, fingers, and legs may indicate neurological deviations. Other inappropriate movements may suggest tics. A tic is a habit spasm or twitching in a small group of muscles. Typical tics involve the eyelid, cheek, lip, and neck muscles. Tics are usually thought to result from anxiety and avoidance responses which later become learned habits.

Appropriate evaluation of these movements and other inappropriate muscle activity should include the time of onset, base rates, area of body involved, and the relationship of the movement to the child's emotional status. Referral for formal psychological investigation of organic involvement may be necessary to determine the presence or absence of brain dysfunction, either of a minimal or more serious nature.

Identifying the onset of various motor activities, including when the child sat alone, crawled, stood alone, and took first steps, will begin to establish developmental patterns. A child will usually walk by twelve months of age and speak in phrases and short sentences by twenty-four months of age. Table II gives a reference to neuromotor and adaptive behavior norms for the first five years of life.

Further evaluation of the child should be based on the number of delays and/or the seriousness of the deficit. If the child, for example, demonstrates three delays in the motor areas or adaptive behavior, then further evaluation is advised. If one or two delays appear so serious as to grossly hinder the child's normal activity, then further evaluation is recommended. Again it must be recalled that the best judgement for delineating delays or development lags is to constantly make comparisons with other children of the same chronological age. It is not uncommon for children to manifest regressions or slowdowns in such developmental stages as walking, talking, and gross and fine motor skills. For example, as the child learns to talk, relapses may occur when a preoccupation with speech is experienced. This behavior is described as the *developmental spiral*. The child progresses forward in one or more areas and regresses in another area (Gesell and Ilg, 1949). Thus, it is not uncommon for young children to develop short-term and minimal speech problems as they progress from an immature to mature status in another area. Developing short relapses in other developmental states is also com-

TABLE II

DEVELOPMENTAL MILESTONES OF NORMAL
INFANTS AND PRE-SCHOOL CHILDREN

Age	Adaptive	Motor
Birth to 4 weeks	Startles to sudden noise. Tracks moving objects with eyes for brief periods.	When placed prone, spontaneously moves head to lateral position. Moves legs alternately to make crawling movements.
By 4 weeks	Tracks moving objects with eyes to or past the midline. Does not grasp objects.	Can hold head erect for a few seconds at most. Hands maintain fisted position. Tonic head reflex position when supine.
By 16 weeks	Will move arms when shown a moving object. Visual following of a moving object is reliably present.	Can balance head in upright position. Postures are typically symmetrical. When prone, spontaneously lifts head to a 90 degree angle.
By 28 weeks	Holds toys with one hand. Can shake a rattle. Can transfer toys from hand to hand.	Can sit if leaning forward supporting with hands. When held upright in standing posture, will bounce.
By 40 weeks	Attempts to scribble in imitation. Can bring 2 objects together at midline.	Sits upright unsupported. Creeps. Can pull to standing.
By 12 months	Will give an object on request.	Stands alone for a short period. Walks if supported by one hand.
By 15 months	Carries out simple commands.	Can creep upstairs. Walks alone with broad based gait.
By 18 months	Spontaneous scribbling. Can build a tower of 3 or 4 blocks. Imitates a line.	Walks with only occasional falling. Can release a ball on throwing. If supported by one hand, can walk upstairs one step at a time.
By 2 years	Imitates both circular and vertical lines. Can build a tower of 6 to 7 blocks.	Can run, go both up and downstairs and kick a large ball.

Age	Adaptive	Motor
By 3 years	Block tower is 9-10 blocks high. Can imitate a bridge using 3 blocks.	Capable of going upstairs using alternate feet, of jumping from a curb or bottom step, and riding a tricycle.
By 4 years	Can copy a cross and possibly a square. Can repeat 4 digits and count 3 objects.	Can walk downstairs using alternate feet. Can stand on one foot up to 4 to 8 seconds.
By 5 years	Can count up to 10 objects. Can copy a square. Can draw a person, with head, body and limbs. May be able to copy a triangle.	Sphincteric control. Able to skip using alternate feet.

Table developed by Stella Chess, M.D. Personal communication, 1976.

mon. If relapses are sustained, a need for further evaluation is indicated. Children who do not establish hand preference are said to characterize lateral confusion. At two years of age, children should begin to demonstrate a preference for their right or left hand. The hand the child consistently uses to reach for things and manipulate objects is considered his/her preference. By preschool age (age three, at the most), if the child does not show definite hand preference and experiences incoordination and clumsiness in motor activities, developmental delays should be considered. At four years of age, signs of lateral confusion normally begin to appear. Lateral confusion is the inability to establish right or left sensory and hand alignment. Essentially, the child should have a definite preference for right or left lateral alignment when performing activities. Some authors suggest that failure to establish dominance will lead to perceptual deficiencies (Gearheart, 1972; Koos, 1964).

One useful test for determining laterality is the Harris Test of Lateral Dominance (1958). On an informal basis, the teacher may ask the child to look through a kaleidoscope, to write his or her name, and to kick a rubber ball. To determine right or left ear preference, a child may be asked to place an ear over the keyhole of a door to listen for noises in the adjoining room. These exercises may be repeated as many times as necessary to determine eye, hand, foot, and ear preference. Right side preference for eye, hand, and foot is an example of proper laterality. Left eye preference and right hand preference are examples of lateral confusion. According to theory, a child should show a definite right or left side preference with eyes, ears, hands, and feet. Should this not occur, lateral confusion is suspected.

It is important not to influence handedness in children by encouraging hand preference. In the event that lateral confusion or mixed dominance begin to surface, this one diagnostic indicator may be suggestive of developmental problems. However, since the research is inconclusive, the teacher should proceed with caution and not make judgements based on only one finding. If other symptoms and developmental deviations begin to surface along with lateral problems, the observations should be included in the referral data.

The teacher should be aware of physical trauma in the child's early years. Head, limb, or torso injury from accidents may be significant in a child's limitations or in the future capability to adjust adequately. The authors are reminded of an example in which a child slipped on his mother's freshly waxed floor and flew headlong into a metal statue. This youngster sustained head injury which resulted in mild but sustained headaches. Obviously, in the large majority of such accidents, injuries are less severe and do not always have permanent qualities.

In other cases involving disfiguration or the functional loss of a limb, a youngster may be unable to accept a handicap and develop psychological problems. Children who contract diabetes sometimes develop emotional problems to the extent that they fail to accept and thus to control their condition. A thorough description of childhood diseases for any child may prove useful. Were there complications from mumps, chicken pox, measles, or the common cold? Did the child run high temperatures for extended periods of time? Less commonly, scarlet fever, heart disorders, tuberculosis, leukemia, and other major diseases may afflict children. In these cases, the severity of impairment, the restriction in behavior, and the youngster's acceptance of the condition should be known. In still other instances, a child may have physical deformities or genetic defects which make adjustment difficult. Where the loss of a limb is concerned, a youngster may develop a very low self-opinion or use the anomaly for secondary gain. For example, a child may constantly search for sympathetic attention and special privileges from adults who view a handicap with feelings of sorrow. Other cases of physical trauma below age five may involve sexual or incestuous attacks from adults; it is always important to know the child's reactions and subsequent adjustment to such events. The most important feature in assessing physical trauma prior to five years of age is to develop an awareness of any factors which may have affected later adjustment. Remediation of trauma necessarily requires a thorough and accurate description of precipitating events.

The teacher should be alert to history where the child appeared to experience definitive memory lapses such as forgetting his or her name, address, or other routines of daily life. Long periods of silence after a child's verbalizations may be suggestive of organic involvement. Further neurological involvement may manifest itself in epileptic seizures. These should be described by type, time of onset, severity, and the probability of future occurrence. All sensory impairments must be clearly described and detailed, such as with hearing and vision. Taking account of full or partial impairments of the visual and auditory modalities will aid the teacher to better understand the child's learning ability and psychological status. It is also becoming increasingly important with the multisensory approaches to learning to make note of any history of kinesthetic or tactile impairments.

Informal investigation of both receptive and expressive language is necessary for early detection of speech and hearing disorders. By the end of eight months the child should have expressed utterances in the forms of laughs and squeals and should display head turning to the sound of a voice. Generally it is expected that a child should vocalize two or more words by one year. Vocalizations usually become associated with physical gestures between twelve and fourteen months. By eighteen months, the child is usually able to name simple objects from pictures and can indicate wants by naming objects such as milk and cookies.

Receptive language refers to the ability of the child to hear and make sense of sounds. By nine months, the child should respond to his or her name and should cease an activity when restrained with "no-no." By eighteen months, hair, mouth, hands, ears, and eyes should be recognized when instructed to point to them. Within twenty-one months, most youngsters can carry out three simple demands, e.g. "put the ball on the chair, then on the table, and then give the ball to me." Within five years, a child should be able to recognize a penny, nickel, and dime. If the child does not pronounce words by three years of age, this may stem from a variety of causes such as hearing loss, infantile autism, mental retardation, or other types of central nervous system dysfunction and/or environmental deprivation. Lack of speech may be caused by elective mutism; that is, the child may choose not to articulate. Such reactions suggest a psychological involvement. Generally, these children selectively articulate in the presence of certain people and not others. Both receptive and expressive language may be evaluated by referring to Table III.

Expressive and receptive language behaviors are given in chronological sequence. The diagnostic instrument may be used informally by referring to the age range appropriate to the child in question and making determinations about language abilities. Where a language deficit is suspected, one should proceed backward chronologically on the chart until a basal age is established. The child's expressive and receptive language sophistication should be determined by establishing the ages by which s/he can perform the various behaviors. In most cases of language impairment, a significant discrepancy will exist between expressive and receptive abilities. A child with prominent verbal nonfluencies is likely to have a much higher receptive language age. Although less common, the youngster with a receptive language disability may be more competent in realizing expressive behaviors. Since most teachers in the school system are not

Table III

LANGUAGE EVALUATION SCALE*

Item	Age	Expressive Language Behavior	Item	Age	Receptive Language Behavior
1	6 mo.	Vocalizes to toys; vocalizes for social contact.	1	6 mo.	Locates source of bell rung out of his sight.
2	7 mo.	Combines vowel sounds m-m-mm when he cries; vocalizes recognition of familiar people.	2	9 mo.	Responds to name or "no-no" (activity ceases).
3	8 mo.	Says "da-da" or "ma-ma" in babbling but not with reference to parents; babbling acquires inflection.	3	10 mo.	Waves "bye-bye" or "patty-cakes" to verbal request.
4	10 mo.	Vocalizes "ma-ma" and "da-da" and has one other "word"; imitates sounds such as cough or tongue click.	4	12 mo.	Comes when called; goes short distances to particular points when directed.
5	12 mo.	Echolalia: imitates a number of syllables as well as sounds. Vocalizes two words other than "mama" and "dada."	5	13 mo.	Give toy on request accompanied by gesture. (Examiner holds out hand for toy child is holding).
6	12–14 mo.	Accompanies gestures by vocalization, e.g. babbles while pointing; spontaneously tries to imitate sounds such as adult exclamation.	6	14 mo.	Recognizes a few objects by name.

*Courtesy of Francis X. Blair, Ph.D., Department of Exceptional Education, The University of Wisconsin, Milwaukee, Wisconsin.

Item	Age	Expressive Language Behavior	Item	Age	Receptive Language Behavior
7	12–14 mo.	Marks with a pencil or crayon; amuses self for brief periods in this way.	7	16 mo.	Recognizes names of a dozen or more familiar objects when he hears them. (And presumably sees them and can point to them.)
8	15 mo.	Has four or five words including names; uses jargon but usually indicates his wants by pointing and vocalizing. Says "tata" or equivalent for "thank you."	8	18 mo.	Recognizes (and points to) hair, mouth, ears, and hands when they are named (Where are your eyes, etc.?)
9	18 mo.	Has a vocabulary of as many as 10 sizeable words; he names "ball" when shown it. May name one picture (dog, shoe, cup, etc.).	9	18 mo.	Throws ball to examiner on request and carries out *two* of the following instructions: "Put it on the chair." "Put it on the table." "Give it to mother." "Give it to me."
10	18 mo.	Asks for wants by naming objects; milk, cookie, etc.	10	18 mo.	Identifies one picture on card. "Show me the dog."
11	18 mo.	Leaves off beginning and ends of phrases; common expression is "all gone."	11	21 mo.	Identifies, by pointing, 3-5 pictures when they are named. Pictures include: dog, cup, shoe, house, flag, clock, star, leaf, basket, book, spoon, comb, and brush.
12	21 mo.	Has vocabulary of 20 words; combines two or three words that express two or more different ideas, e.g. "daddy go bye-bye" (not just "go bye-bye"); echoes two or more last words.	12	18–21 mo.	Points to parts of a doll on request—finds one part at 18 months and an additional part for each succeeding month up to 22 months.

Item	Age	Expressive Language Behavior	Receptive Language Behavior	Age	Item
13	21–24 mo.	Expressive vocabulary of at least 25 words; mostly nouns, some verbs, adverbs and adjectives; uses names of several familiar objects spontaneously and not merely when they are presented; talks in short sentences or phrases or subject-object combinations in a practically useful way.	Carries out *three* instructions with the ball (See item #9)	21 mo.	13
14	2 yr.	Vocabulary may exceed 50 words; jargon is discarded in favor of understandable but simple *three word sentences*; uses pronouns "I," "me," and "you" although not always correctly. He soliloquizes, verbalizing his immediate experience, referring to himself by name ("Johnny fall down," etc.) Common expressions "mine" (me).	Carries out *four* instructions with the ball (See item #9).	24 mo.	14
15	2 yr.	Names three or more common pictures such as those found in a Golden Book Dictionary; names as he leafs through book.	Identifies five or more *pictures*.	24 mo.	15
16	2 yr.	Verbalizes for food, drink, and toilet. Asks for "another _____," wanting one for each hand.	"Look at," "Show me," "Give me," spoon, comb, hairbrush, shoe, cup. (life-size objects)	24 mo.	16
16a	2–6 yr.	(repeats two digits) See Receptive Language.			

Item	Age	Expressive Language Behavior	Receptive Language Behavior	Age	Item
17	2–6 yr.	Gives his full name.	Identifies seven *pictures*. (See item #11).	2–6 yr.	17
18	2–6 yr.	Gives use of some of the test objects (ball, shoe, penny, pencil, etc.). Names test objects: shoe, watch, telephone, flag, pack knife.	Understands "just one block." Selects one block from group in response to "Give me just one block."	2–6 yr.	18
19	2–6 yr.	Refers to self by pronouns rather than by name.	Recognizes objects by function 1. "Show me what we drink out of." "Show me what we buy candy with." "Show me what goes on our feet." "Show me what we can cut with." "Show me what we ride in." "Show me what we use to iron clothes."	2–6 yr. (3 or more)	19
20	2–6 yr.	Speech activities are repetitive.	Repeats two digits: "Listen; say 2. Now say_____." 4-7 6-3 5-8	2–6 yr.	20
21	2–6 yr.	Common expression is "I did."	Recognizes objects by function 2. "Show me the one that . . . . a) we cook on b) we sleep in (bed) c) a man smokes (pipe) d) we sit on (chair) e) we sweep the dust into (dustpan) f) we cut with (scissors)	2–6 yr. (4+)	21

Item	Age	Expressive Language Behavior	Item	Age	Receptive Language Behavior
22	3 yr.	Vocabulary has innumerable words; he speaks in well-formed simple sentences.	22	2–6 yr.	Size Concept: Two teaspoons, one doll spoon. (Place perpendicular to child's line of vision, doll spoon in middle) "Look at this one, and that one and this one." "Show me the tiny little spoon."
23	3 yr.	Uses some plurals.	23	2–6 yr.	Recognizes pictures by function. (Spoon, comb, shoe) "Listen carefully. Show me the the picture of the thing we use to eat our cereal." "Which thing does mother need to fix your hair?" "Can you find something that goes on your foot?"
24	3 yr.	Names pictures, and on request tells the action, e.g. "baby is sleeping."	24	2–6/3 yr.	Identifies action in pictures. "Show me the boy (girl) . . . a. walking b. running c. jumping d. sitting
25	3 yr.	Knows a few rhymes. (Little Bo-Peep, Miss Muffet, etc.)	25	2–6/3 yr.	Recognition of action in image (two 10 x 6 colored pictures of children sleeping in bed and eating at a table). "Look at these nice pictures." "Where (show me) are the children sleeping in their beds?" "Show me where the children are eating their dinner."
25a	3 yr.	Copies circle; imitates cross.			
25b	3 yr.	Repeats three digits. (See Receptive Language).			

Item	Age	Expressive Language Behavior	Item	Age	Receptive Language Behavior
26	3 yr.	Names eight pictures correctly (cup, kitty, shoe, house, flag, clock, star, leaf, basket, book)	26	3 yr.	Repeats one series of 3 digits "Say 4-2. Now say . . ." 6-4-1 3-5-2 8-3-7
27	3 yr.	Tells sex correctly in response to "are you a little boy or a little girl."	27	3 yr.	Comprehension of one question. "What must you do when you are sleepy?" (hungry, cold)
28	3 yr. 3–6	Relates experiences. Gives simple accounts of experiences or tells stories (unprompted) with sequential and coherent content and relevant detail.	28	3 yr.	Preposition directions (must respond to at least two) "Put the ball . . . a. on the chair b. under the chair c. in front of the chair d. beside the chair e. back of the chair
29	3–6/4 yr.	Names all primary colors when shown.	29	3–0/3–6 yr.	Interpretation of pictures (Same pictures as in Item #25) "Look at these two pictures. See what they are doing here and here." "Which one tells you (or "makes you think") that it is night time?"
30	3–6/4 yr.	Vocabulary in excess of 1500 words.	30	3–6 yr. (3 out of 3)	Comparison of sticks (2" stick) (2½" stick) "Which stick is longer?" a. _____ b. _____ c. _____

Item	Age	Expressive Language Behavior	Item	Age	Receptive Language Behavior
31	4 yr.	Counts three objects, pointing to each in turn.	31	3–6 yr. (3 out of 3)	Comparison of balls (2 cut out circles) "Which ball is bigger?"
31a	4 yr.	Names objects from memory (See Receptive Language).			
32	4 yr. (2+)	Memory for sentences. Say "big boy." Now say, "I am a big boy." Now say, a. I like to eat ice cream cones. b. My watch has two hands. c. Give me just one of them.	32	4 yr.	Comprehension of these questions "What must you do when you are: sleepy, hungry, cold?"
33	4/4–6 yr.	Reads and tells a familiar story by way of pictures ("Three Bears," etc.).	33	4 yr.	Naming objects from memory. Place 3 objects in a row before the child. Ask him to name each (if he cannot, examiner should do so.) Screen the objects with a board and cover one object with box. "Which did I hide?" (suggested objects: auto, dog, shoe, cat, spoon, locomotive, doll, scissors, thimble, box.)
33a	4–6 yr.	Repeats four digits. (See Receptive Language).			
34	4–6/5 yr.	Prints simple words such as first name or a few familiar words not using copy. Correct spelling not essential.	34	4 yr.	Carries out four individual commands using prepositions. (see item #28)
35	5 yr.	Counts 10 objects, pointing to each in turn.	35	4 yr. (3+)	Object identification through function "Show me the one: a. we cook on b. we carry when its raining c. that gives us milk d. that we read e. that grows on a tree f. that the hen lays

Item	Age	Expressive Language Behavior	Item	Age	Receptive Language Behavior
36	5 yr.	Gives a descriptive comment while naming the objects in a composite picture.	36	4 yr. (2+)	Number Concept of 2 a. Put 2 blocks in front of 5 blocks. Ask, "How many?" b. Remove blocks and present 2 square beads, asking "How many?" c. Remove beads and place 4 beads before 5 and say, "Give me 2 beads and you take 2."
37	5–5/6 yr.	Relates fanciful tales: tells an experience of plan of action which is imaginative only.	37	4 yr. (2+)	Opposite analogies. Say: a. Brother is a boy; sister is a _____ . b. In daytime it is light; at night it is _____ . c. Father is a man; mother is a _____ . d. The snail is slow; the rabbit is _____ . e. The sun shines during the day; the moon at _____ .
38	5–5/6 yr.	Names penny, nickel, dime: asks for them discriminately for varying purposes.	38	4 yr. (2+)	Comprehension a. Why do we have houses? b. Why do we have books?
38a	5–5/6 yr.	Memory for sentences (See Receptive Language).			
39	5–5/6 yr.	Can count to 30 by ones upon request; does not need help after beginning to count.	39	4–6 yr.	Repeating 4 digits. "I am going to say some numbers and when I am through, I want you to say them just the way I do. Listen carefully and get them just right." a. 4-7-2-9 b. 3-8-5-2 c. 7-2-6-1

Item	Age	Expressive Language Behavior	Item	Age	Receptive Language Behavior
40	5–5/6 yr.	Asks meaning of words: "What does _____ mean?" Or a similar question.	40	4–6 yr. (2+)	"What is a _____ made of?" a. chair b. dress c. shoe
			41	4–6 yr. (2+)	Opposite Analogies a. Brother is a boy; sister is a _____. b. A table is made of wood; a window is made of _____. c. A bird flies; a fish _____. d. The point of a cane is blunt; the point of a knife is _____. e. An inch is short; a mile is _____.
			42	4–6 yr. (1+) 5 yr. (2+)	Comprehension a. "What do we do with our eyes?" b. "What do we do with our ears?"
			43	5 yr.	Can identify (point to) on request: a. penny b. nickel c. dime
			44	5 yr. (2+)	Number concept of three a. Give me three blocks. b. Give me three beads. c. Give me two blocks and one bead.
			45	5 yr.	Can identify four colors

Item	Age	Expressive Language Behavior	Item	Age	Receptive Language Behavior
			46	5 yr.	Carries out, in order, a command containing three parts, e.g. "Pick up the ball, put it on the table, and bring me the book."
			47	5 yr.	Definitions. a. "What is a ball?" b. "What is a hat?" c. "What is a stove?"
			48	5 yr. (2+)	Memory for sentences. "I want you to say something for me. Say "big boy (or girl)." Now say "I am a big boy (or girl)." Now say . . . a. "Jane wants to build a big castle in her playhouse." b. "Tom has lots of fun playing ball with his sister."
			49	5 yr. (2+)	Counting four objects. Present the objects in a row in following series: a. 4 blocks b. 4 beads c. 4 pennies

trained as speech clinicians, referral to appropriate specialists should be made when puzzling speech and language problems are identified.

Bowel or bladder incontinence is not uncommon among preschool children. If the child is demonstrating lack of fecal or urine retention by the fourth year or beginning of preschool, it is important for the teacher to suggest referral for a medical examination. If these findings are negative, a referral for a psychological evaluation is essential. The causal factors for such reactions are varied. It is not unusual for a parent to describe the use of severe discipline during toilet training. Starting toilet training too early with an immature nervous system may result in prolonged incontinence (Heinstein, 1966; Sears, Maccoby, and Levin, 1957).

AFFECTIVE DEVELOPMENT

Affective development of the child occurs through a learning process. Children who are extremely retarded or autistic are slow to acquire appropriate and spontaneous affective responses. By one month, the child is expected to show excitement as indicated by whole body movements or the infant moving in an "all or none fashion." As the infant grows older, affective development becomes differentiated from excitement into other emotions as with expressions of distress, delight, fear, anger, elation, and affection. By examining Figure 1, the teacher can readily distinguish how emotions become differentiated and more complex from birth to five years of age.

By studying the various emotions displayed in Figure 1, the teacher may use the outline as an informal instrument for determining if a child has displayed appropriate emotionality at various ages. The figure is especially helpful in identifying both positive and negative emotions at appropriate chronological ages. Any gross emotional deviation, such as lack of excitement at two years, may indicate serious developmental deficiencies. If unchecked, such deficits may later result in numerous behavioral and emotional problems in late childhood. Finding that gross discrepancies in emotional development existed before the child

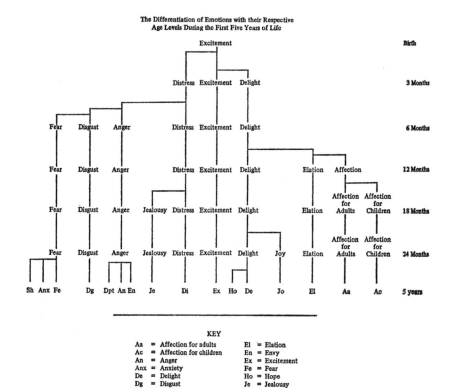

Figure 1. From Bridges, K. M. B., Emotional development in early infancy. *Child Development,* 3:324-341, 1932. Courtesy of The Society for Research in Child Development, Inc.

reached school age will give the teacher helpful hints as to various means for approaching the deficiencies, such as encouraging parental involvement in a remediation program. The teacher should also take note of the child who has reportedly lacked emotional warmth and fails to show sensitivity and affection for others.

Excessive tantrums, stubbornness, negativism, and breath holding may be attention-arousing devices. Another child may be characterized by a history of excessive and prolonged crying which results from minimal environmental stress. The child characterized by excessive shyness or timidity may have shown early signs of a personality disorder. Excessive fears of non-threatening stimuli such as cats, birds, other children, or inclement weather are further indications of emotional problems.

Additional developmental irregularities of emotions may occur through excessive anxiety demonstrated by body tremors, dryness of the mouth, and frequent urination. Reactions commonly referred to as "anxiety attacks" usually result from the child being overwhelmed by excessive stress. The attacks by themselves are not serious but suggest that the child is experiencing intense anxiety. A psychological referral and subsequent remediation program should be implemented.

Excessive tension is associated with insecurity and feelings of inadequacy and can be manifested by children in a variety of forms. Children sometimes display excessive finger sucking and chewing on clothing. When this sucking behavior persists into the preschool years and is performed frequently during the day, it should be considered maladaptive. Frequently associated with excessive mouthing is chewing shirt collars or other articles of clothing or objects. Some children need a security object such as a blanket or small stuffed animal like a teddy bear, monkey, or rabbit. The child usually sleeps with these articles and may carry them during the day. This is maladaptive only in extreme form or when the child prefers this object to people.

Many children go through a phase when they show excessive attachment to a person, animal, or object. The behavior becomes maladaptive when the activity is prolonged and is demanded during such inappropriate occasions as mealtime and play activities with the peer group. Another sign of insecurity may be nail-biting, which is excessive by anyone's standards when the ends of the fingers bleed. Some children experiencing high anxiety also manifest various facial contortions, especially when they try to verbally express themselves. Such expressions are maladaptive when they hinder communication.

The teacher must be alert to the child who is described as being overexcitable to a minimal stimulus, which in turn may cause frequent crying. Similarly, there is the young disturbed child who cries or becomes elated for no apparent reason and whose responses are inappropriate to the situation. Lack of acceptance may initiate a host of inappropriate emotional and behavioral responses in children. Such maladaptive behaviors as explosiveness, threatening physical violence to an infant sibling, and screaming until hoarse must be recorded by the teacher if s/he becomes aware of the information.

Autism

In rare situations, the preschool or sometimes elementary school teacher might identify a child who is severely disturbed and unable to become involved in the most attractive classroom activities. Childhood autism is a thinking disorder accompanied by a number of symptoms. Although there is a great deal of question as to the etiology of childhood autism, it usually refers to distorted and self-centered thinking which bears little relationship to objective reality. For normal children, such thinking is similar to fantasy; with autistic youngsters, it occurs almost constantly. Autism refers to behavior that is manifested by bizarre verbal and motor responding, echolalia, language deficiencies, obsessiveness, and a constricted and narrow range of behavior (Kanner, 1965).

If autism is suspected, there are many other signs that the teacher should investigate which are accurate diagnostic indicators. These include aloofness from early infant cuddling, absence of or limited speech, ignoring of other people, self-stimulating activities such as hitting themselves and sometimes damaging body parts from blows by the hands or throwing themselves, avoidance of direct eye contact, lack of expressive emotionality, object rather than person preference, and sustained utterances such as screeches or yells.

It is very difficult to obtain an IQ on these children with standard individual intelligence tests. Research suggests, however, that many of these children are of average intelligence (Rutter and Bartak, 1971).

It is helpful to remember that childhood autism is an extreme disorder of thinking or bizarre responding and may or may not have major organic components. These children should be referred for a formal evaluation to the school mental health specialist. The prognosis for complete remediation of autistic symptoms is questionable; however, with early recognition, the probability of symptom remission is greater than if it is not recognized until later elementary years.

Child Abuse

The last major area of the affective assessment considers child abuse. The abused child requires some special identification efforts on the part of the teacher. In its broadest sense, child abuse includes any problems resulting from lack of reasonable care and protection by the child's caretakers. It can be physical abuse, nutritional neglect, sexual abuse, health care neglect, or emotional abuse. The law requires physicians to report suspected child abuse cases to child protective services agencies in all fifty states. The teacher also has a responsibility for detection and reporting of suspected abuse incidents. According to most estimates, two thirds of all child abuse cases occur during the first three years of life. Therefore, the relevance of this topic is especially important in investigating the developmental history of the first five years of life.

Some of the more common types of physical abuse include bruises, cigarette burns, head injuries, and bone fractures. If evidence of physical abuse is suspected, a teacher should document the evidence as objectively and thoroughly as possible so that a claim could be supported, especially since testimony would probably be required at a later time. A school nurse is helpful in charting such data, and photographs of any physically visible injuries are exceptionally helpful. Some injuries are especially difficult to identify, such as those to the middle ear and the internal abdominal cavity. Others are more obvious, such as eye damage, open wounds, and telltale marks from belt buckles and hot water scalds. When bruises, lacerations, and fractures are multiple, the evidence is especially indicative of child abuse. In discussing a child's developmental history, the parent who is willing to talk about previous incidents of abuse is most often the parent who has been able to recognize the problem and get professional help. On the other hand, the parent who speaks in vague and contradictory terms about a child's old injuries may be trying to deny his or her behavior as an abusing parent. When there are gross discrepancies about injuries in the child's developmental history, in addition to evidence of physical abuse as the child comes to school, a teacher can suspect a history of child mistreatment.

Nutritional neglect is difficult to identify, since it is commonly associated with cultural deprivation and poverty life-styles. With babies, the main cause of this disorder is simply that the child is not fed enough. In such instances, it is frequently the case that such a child was unwanted. It is also sometimes the case that an underfed child is in the home of a single parent who feels trapped and unfairly responsible to the baby. If this kind of information surfaces in taking a developmental history from a parent, specific evidence of dehydration and malnutrition without obvious cause should be observed.

It is commonly believed that sexual abuse of children is the most undiagnosed variety of child abuse. Evidence of vaginal tract infections, venereal diseases, and physical damage to sexual organs is occasionally reported in children of a very young age and should naturally lead to suspicions of sexual abuse. This kind of situation is most commonly perpetrated by an adult male who is not a blood relative of the female child. Such abuse is difficult to identify, although teachers should make note of its occurrence if a parent volunteers the information in a history. By the same token, if a teacher suspects that sexual abuse is occurring to one of his/her students, based on comments related to the teacher, it should be carefully considered and recorded with as much direct quoting as possible.

Health care neglect is also a difficult kind of abuse to document because it is most commonly based on whether a parent used poor judgement about a particular medical malady. If parents consistently ignore medical recommendations while a child's health deteriorates, there is cause for outside intervention on either the part of protective services or the courts. If health care neglect is reported in the process of taking a developmental history, the teacher may wish to look for lasting physical defects which may have resulted from failure to treat a condition. A glaring example would be a child who is not receiving insulin and whose condition remains brittle and subject to fluctuations in blood sugar reactions.

Emotional abuse may be the single greatest example of child abuse. Extremes may exist from less than obvious parental rejection to periodic abandoning of a child. Other more common forms include verbal attack, ridicule, terrorizing, and denying children opportunities for normal psychological growth by constantly confining their activities to their rooms. This kind of abuse is difficult to reverse and requires some long-term commitment to psychotherapy on the part of the parents. Children who have been so abused are often characterized as insecure, fearful, grossly uneasy around unfamiliar adults, withdrawn, and, in its most severe form, autistic. The emotionally abused child is frequently an unwanted child who comes from a home that lacks nurturance, warmth, and affection. This kind of abuse is difficult to identify and record, and every attempt must be made by the observer to be as objective as possible.

If child abuse has occurred during the first five years of life, it will typically only be mentioned in a developmental history-taking if the parent has found some help for this inadequacy and feels comfortable in the progress that has been made. If parents have not sought help for their abusing tendencies, there is usually a consistent effort to deny any possibility of child abuse and to make excuses for neglect, injury, and deprivation in the past. The more supportive and nonjudgmental a teacher can be in the process of discussing such sensitive material, the greater the potential for processing a referral to deal with such a problem. If current child abuse is suspected, the teacher should share the information with the administrative superiors and it should then be passed along to the appropriate child protective agency. When child abuse is only of historical interest after the family problems causing it have been remediated, teachers should draw as little attention to it as possible unless it has some obvious bearing on present problem situations.

CASE STUDY IV

Teacher's Report (David C., 4 years old, preschool)

David has been attending the Clark preschool for the past two and one half months. He has been described by his teachers as being bright, alert to the responses of his peers, vocal, extremely active, and curious. He is popular with his peers and shows many leadership qualities. During the first ten weeks of school, David did not show any obvious learning, social, or emotional difficulties. He did, however, occasionally state that his mother and father argued a great deal. Within the last two weeks, on three different occasions, he did not want to leave the Clark preschool when it was time to go home. He occupied himself with building blocks and indicated that he wished to complete his projects prior to leaving. On one of these situations, the teacher aide had to bodily lift and place him in the family car with his mother. It was also noticed by the preschool personnel that his mother had never made an on-site visit to the school. This was obvious because other parents frequently made visits and were curious about their child's activities. About the time David indicated reluctance to return home it was noticed that he had slight bruises on his right arm and right side of his face. When questioned about these marks, he indicated that his mother had hit him and pushed him down the basement stairs. At a meeting with the preschool staff, the teacher, Mrs. Jones, related the above. It was suggested by the preschool principal that since the child's arm bruises were not extensive, the school would have to proceed carefully in determining a case for child abuse.

Suggested Alternatives

1. Refer the child to the local social and rehabilitation services which deal with child abuse.
2. Refer the child to the family physician.
3. Wait for a longer period of time in order to accumulate more clear-cut evidence.
4. Request the parent to give some information relative to the bruises on the child's right side.

Recommended Solution (David C., 4 years old, preschool)

To choose alternative 3 and wait to observe if more detailed and elaborate bruises occur may potentially expose the child to greater abuse. In most cases of child abuse, there is always the question about the extensiveness and intensity of the bruises or other signs of neglect that the child may be experiencing. It is not suggested here that every child should be referred when tiny bruises are found. Many mild injuries occur in typical playtime activities. In this case, however, the child stated that his mother had pushed him down the stairs and prior to that had indicated that there was a great deal of arguing within the home situation. These two situations suggest that there is some type of child neglect present. Such evidence is supported by the fact that this child did not previously show psychological, emotional, social, or interaction difficulties. In fact, he was considered bright and showed many leadership qualities. Furthermore, it is also of particular interest that the child only recently indicated reluctance to going home. To report the findings to the family physician is a likely alternative, although all fifty states have a child abuse reporting system, and it is better to communicate with these specialists as they are trained in this area. Furthermore, the physician may not want to become involved. Thus, to seek alternative 1 is the most likely, as this delivery system is prepared to investigate and obtain more elaborate information on the details of the potential child abuse. Alternative 4 has several assets and liabilities. The liabilities are simply that the parents may lie, become defensive, and, as a result, withdraw the child from school. On the other hand, the parents may indicate a very simple reason for the bruises which is logical and rational. However, it is not the purpose of the teacher to make a diagnosis, and under such conditions alternative 1 is supported, since these professionals are prepared to educate the public as well as investigate the seriousness of the situation.

SOCIAL DEVELOPMENT

Social development is assessed through information on how the child interacts with his peers, siblings, parents, and others. The best indicators of a child in need of special assistance is revealed through his/her social interactions. Problem behaviors will expose themselves in terms of the child interacting or not interacting with peers, teachers, parents, and others within their social context. Problem behaviors will become evident through the way the child relates to objects, in attempts to resolve conflict situations, and by participation in classroom activities. By investigating early interpersonal difficulties, current social functioning may be understood. Carefully noting the age of playmates as well as the usual type of play is important. Major forms of play activity can be seen as the child moves from solitary to parallel to cooperative play. In solitary play, the child enjoys entertainment away from others, while in parallel play the child engages in independent activity alongside other children but does not become involved with them. Sharing in an organized interactive fashion is labeled cooperative play. Excessive solitary play over a prolonged period of time in a preschool setting, when associated with detachment and withdrawal, can be a symptom of a more serious adjustment difficulty.

It is also useful to know a child's leadership role in his peer group or the extent to which the role of follower is assumed. The child who possesses leadership qualities will innovate activities and encourage other children to participate in a cooperative fashion. Some children will resist another child's leadership role by rebelliousness and reluctance to participate. It is not the participation in the activity that actually bothers them but the emerging leadership of another child. These subtle conflicts do not suggest, for the most part, problem behaviors, but should they be carried to the extreme, the teacher may need to intervene. However, the research on leadership in small children offers no conclusive evidence about its transferability into adolescence and adulthood.

Excessive attachment to one parent or peer to the exclusion of others may indicate faulty parenting or may point to pathological social development in the child. Likewise, children who prefer objects and things to people are probably expressing some fear of intimacy. Such a child may feel threatened by physical and emotional closeness to people and may reject the formation of personal relationships. Other children are known to be oversuggestible, to lie or exaggerate excessively, to isolate themselves from peers, or to tattle as a means of inviting acceptance.

The teacher should be alert to extreme negativism, refusal to participate in activities and expected routines, and resistance to authority figures in the early developmental history. The teacher should be aware of the child who has exhibited extreme shyness and who lacks desire to become interactively involved with other

TABLE IV

EXPECTED BEHAVIORS ACCORDING TO AGE LEVELS*

Age level 0-1

1. "Crows"—laughs
2. Balances head
3. Grasps objects within reach
4. Reaches for familiar persons
5. Rolls over
6. Reaches for nearby objects
7. Occupies self unattended
8. Sits unsupported
9. Pulls self upright
10. "Talks"—imitates sounds
11. Drinks from cup or glass assisted
12. Moves about on floor
13. Grasps with thumb and finger
14. Demands personal attention
15. Stands alone
16. Does not drool
17. Follows simple instructions

Age level 1-2

18. Walks about room unattended
19. Marks with pencil or crayon
20. Masticates food
21. Pulls off socks
22. Transfers objects
23. Overcomes simple obstacles
24. Fetches or carries familiar objects
25. Drinks from cup or glass unassisted
26. Gives up baby carriage
27. Plays with other children
28. Eats with spoon
29. Goes about house or yard
30. Discriminates edible substances
31. Uses names of familiar objects
32. Walks upstairs unassisted
33. Unwraps candy
34. Talks in short sentences

Age level 2-3

35. Asks to go to toilet
36. Initiates own play activities
37. Removes coat or dress
38. Eats with fork
39. Gets drink unassisted
40. Dries own hands
41. Avoids simple hazards
42. Puts on coat or dress unassisted
43. Cuts with scissors
44. Relates experiences

Age level 3-4

45. Walks downstairs one step per tread
46. Plays cooperatively at kindergarten level
47. Buttons coat or dress
48. Helps at little household tasks
49. "Performs" for others
50. Washes hands unaided

Age level 4-5

51. Cares for self at toilet
52. Washes face unassisted
53. Goes about neighborhood unattended
54. Dresses self except for tying
55. Uses pencil or crayon for drawing
56. Plays competitive exercise games

Age level 5-6

57. Uses skates, sled, wagon
58. Prints simple words
59. Plays simple table games
60. Is trusted with money
61. Goes to school unattended

* From Doll, E. A. Vineland Social Maturity Scale. Circle Pines, Minn.: American Guidance Services, Inc., 1965.

children. Excessive verbal or physical aggressiveness may be manifested by the child who has frequent conflicts with other children. This suggests poor or inadequate socialization.

Table IV lists social development behaviors which the teacher may use for determining the appropriateness of a young child's action. This table is intended to give the teacher informal measures of social behaviors from the first few months of life through five years of age. By continually making comparison judgements between children and being aware of expected behaviors according to age levels, the teacher will become readily equipped to identify behaviors of youngsters who are in need of special attention.

Items from Table IV are useful social indicators and add to the thoroughness of informal assessment. If evidence of social developmental delays or lags surface in the process of informal assessment, then referral for formalized testing may be needed. Experience with numbers of children will make teachers aware of when critical stages of social learning were missed. Generally, one or two areas of delay is not considered pathognomonic, while clusters of delayed responses may be.

The teacher should also be aware of cultural differences and lack of environmental stimulation when assessing social development in small children. For example, it was not uncommon in the early days of integrated public schools for black ghetto children to be unfamiliar with social behaviors expected by their white middle-class teachers. Remediation of impoverished social behavior must take into account the child's developmental history. Otherwise it cannot be known if a child's deficits are familial, cultural, or intellectually based, whether they are short term or historical in nature, and whether the child has displayed ability to overcome deficits in the past.

SUGGESTED READINGS

Poteet, J. A.: *Behavior Modification: A Practical Guide for Teachers.* Minneapolis, Minn. Burgess Publishing Co., 1973.
This book will assist in effectively describing and measuring

normal behaviors of young children. Although the emphasis is on changing behaviors, it provides excellent examples for teachers to describe various behaviors prior to the use of behavior modification. It also gives methods for measuring, graphing, and forming baseline data of target behavior.

Hurlock, E. B.: *Developmental Psychology,* 3rd ed. New York, McGraw-Hill, 1968.

This book provides a thorough and sophisticated background into the development of young children through adult life. Throughout the text are examples of various behavior expected at different ages, and some norms are provided for making comparison judgments between children. This book will be particularly helpful because of the way it emphasizes the social and psychological developmental aspects of early childhood. It will serve as an excellent resource for gaining in-depth evaluation of the developmental processes in young children.

Haring, N. G. (Ed.): *Behavior of Exceptional Children: An Introduction to Special Education.* Columbus, Ohio, Charles E. Merrill, 1974.

The first five sections of this book are devoted to understanding special education in young children. It is an excellent resource for ascertaining developmental norms in children up to and through preschool age. The whole impact of the book is on the characteristics and educational resources of exceptional or atypical children. It also provides a good historical basis by which to gain an understanding of exceptional children prior to preschool and through elementary school.

Chapter 3

Brain Dysfunctions

Chapter Objectives

- *Four symptoms of an organically based impairment of an elementary school child which might be confused with a learning disability or perceptual handicap.*
- *Five basic behavioral symptoms of minimal brain dysfunction which may be readily observed in a classroom setting.*
- *Four characteristics which are suggestive of petit mal seizure disorder and the means by which a petit mal disorder may be distinguished from an attention disorder which characterizes a learning-disabled youngster.*
- *The informal assessment of the following learning and perceptual problems:*
  a. visual figure-ground
  b. auditory sequential memory
  c. visual sequential memory
  d. auditory recognition
  e. visual recognition
  f. visual closure
  g. auditory localization
- *Five characteristics which are suggestive of the hyperkinetic syndrome in children.*
- *Three basic patterns which characterize perseverative activity manifested within a child.*

SOME EDUCATORS FEEL that it is not the place of the school to identify brain disorders, that investigation of brain disorders should be left to the family physician. On the other hand, many symptoms of brain dysfunctions are subtle, and the best observer of these problems is the person who has routine contact with children on a daily basis. Diagnosis of subtle problems typically cannot be done in two yearly visits to a physician's office. The counselor, school psychologist, and teacher interact with children on a daily basis and have continuous contact with them. They, therefore, can become more expert observers of comprehensive behavior patterns. Over time, by observing children interacting with their peer group, these professionals are in the best position to make subtle comparisons of behavior and academic performance and, as a result, to identify potential problems. Furthermore, if children are not recognized within the school environment as having brain disorders, many may never be treated.

Investigation and observation concerning this area are intended to determine if the child is experiencing brain disorder symptoms. Such impairments may cause the child to experience personality alterations, poor academic performance, and social interaction difficulties. Often the behavioral and personality symptoms of brain disorders and psychologically caused problems are similar. Brain dysfunctions frequently produce psychological symptoms, but psychological symptoms generally do not produce brain pathology. If brain pathology exists and the child is treated by counseling or educational therapy for these symptoms, nonproductive consequences will result. For instance, the child who shows poor gross motor coordination by tripping and awkward running and who also has psychological symptoms of low frustration tolerance and poor self-concept may, in fact, be suffering from organic impairment. Psychological or educational remediation may be necessary for these symptoms, but not before a determination about the organic involvement is made. An example may help clarify this point. One youngster was referred to a third-grade learning disability classroom because of poor writing quality and awkward gross motor coordination skills. She also complained of frequent headaches, and the pupils of her eyes were unevenly dilated. The latter two symptoms were completely neglected, and no investigation was made into the origin of her fine and gross motor deficiencies. A conversation with her first-grade teacher revealed that there were no indications of physical awkwardness and that her writing quality was average. Her second-grade teacher noticed that the child's mood was capricious but attributed this condition to the home. It was only after progressive failure during the last two months of the school year in the learning disability classroom that the teacher and principal considered the probability of an active organic dysfunction. Sometime during the following summer, an intracranial neoplasm was identified and surgically removed. In retrospect, the symptoms of an organically based impairment were obvious. Had the child been appropriately evaluated, both psychologically and medically, as warranted by the presented symptomatology for her deteriorating course, many of the resulting problems could likely have been avoided through early diagnosis and treatment.

When evaluating a child's behavioral and intellectual functioning, it is important to recognize some of the more common symptoms characterizing both the major and minimal types of brain dysfunctions. The following discussion will center upon diagnostic indicators of brain dysfunctions.

DIAGNOSTIC INDICATORS OF BRAIN DYSFUNCTIONS

Clements (1966) offers a descriptive guide for comparing various brain disorders. He has divided brain dysfunctions on a scale ranging from minimal to severe. The minimal brain dysfunctions refer to subtle neurological differences which result in deviations of coordination, attention, activity, affect, and perceptual impairments. These symptoms are not readily apparent, but they typically characterize the child with learning problems, hyperactivity, and perceptual disorders. On the other hand, the characteristics of the major brain dysfunctions are overt; and among their manifestations are cerebral palsy, epilepsy, and the major sensory impairments (blindness, deafness, etc.). The symptoms of cerebral palsy and sensory impairments will not be discussed, as they are almost always recognized by parents and medical personnel prior to the time the child enters kindergarten or first grade. Attention will be centered upon the diagnostic indicators of epilepsies and all symptoms of the minimal brain dysfunctions. If present, these symptoms should be recognized before formal educational assessment of the child. Furthermore, it is these symptoms that the family physician typically does not recognize, therefore, the school environment is the best situation for their identification.

Epilepsies

The four major types of epilepsies are grand mal, petit mal, psychomotor, and focal motor. Although there are four main types of epilepsies, grand mal and petit mal are significantly more likely to occur in children and adolescents.

In one half to two thirds of the occurrences, a grand mal (major motor) seizure is preceded by an aura. An aura is a sense or feeling that has come to be recognized as a warning that a seizure is about to occur. The grand mal seizure disorder is composed of convulsive muscular movements, usually with tonic and clonic components, which last from approximately two to four minutes. In conjunction with the convulsive motor component, the grand mal seizure is always associated with loss of consciousness and is usually accompanied by rolling back of the eyes. Some children may experience bowel and bladder incontinence, visceral disturbances, increased salivation, and tongue biting. Depending upon the duration of the tonic motor phase, they may also evidence cyanosis of varying degree. Following the motor component, with resumption of respiration and clearing of the cyanosis, the child will be unconscious for variable periods of time ranging from a few minutes to one-half hour. On regaining consciousness, the victim usually experiences confusion, lack of orientation, drowsiness, and generalized muscle ache with associated fatigue and headaches (Keith, 1963).

The petit mal type is frequently referred to as an "absence attack" and is most commonly manifested by a vacant stare during a brief period of suspended consciousness ("absence"). Other petit mal symptoms may include eyelid fluttering, slight muscular twitching about the face, and release of hand grip (akinesis). Some children may suddenly slump or fall to the floor from generalized relaxation of muscles (atonia). The attack generally lasts a matter of seconds but may in rare instances extend up to a minute. Petit mal seizures are limited almost exclusively to children, primarily between the ages of four and twelve, and almost without exception disappear as the individual progresses through early adolescence. A significant percentage (approaching 50 percent) experience conversion of grand mal or psychomotor seizures after clearing of the petit mal disorder (Rodin, 1968). One good indicator of absence attacks (petit mal) is a teacher's complaints that the child is not attentive and seems to be preoccupied by "inner thoughts." It is interesting to note that although awareness is briefly lost by the child, postural control is nearly always maintained. Attention should be given to the duration and frequency of the seizure. Upon inquiry, most of these children will note that they were not daydreaming and will usually reveal their lack of awareness of having had an attack. Children may experience up to 200 attacks per day (Bridge, 1949).

It is not unusual for teachers and some mental health specialists to confuse this kind of problem with a functional disorder of attention. In rare instances, the attacks are so frequent that the "absences," with the attending effect on learning, lead to erroneously viewing the child as mentally defective. In such cases, it would be unjust to modify what is believed to be excessive daydreaming or inattentiveness with the use of behavior modification techniques. If the teacher suspects petit mal seizures, a referral for neurological evaluation should be made, with a detailed description of the observed traits. With proper training, the teacher is in the best position to identify the symptoms of petit mal seizures.

Although less common in children, focal seizures, when motor in type, are similar to the tonic-clonic phase of grand mal seizures. As suggested by the name, however, they are characterized by focal or localized involvement, at least with onset of the attack. In most instances, the seizure first becomes evident in one portion of the body, e.g. a finger, foot, or a part of the face, and progresses in a marching or gradual fashion to involve the entire side of the body. As is quite often the case, it may suddenly spread to the other side; the seizure is then associated with loss of consciousness and development of a generalized major motor seizure. The focal seizure which spreads progressively from an isolated onset to adjacent areas within the brain by igniting the associated cortical representation of the body parts is known as a Jacksonian seizure. Some individuals do not lose consciousness because the seizure discharge does not spread to the other side and involve the whole brain.

The psychomotor seizure is characterized by bizarre and inappropriate behavior (psychological and motor), while motor function remains essentially intact. These behaviors may take the form of removing one's clothing, throwing violent tantrums, or inappropriately running around a room. On observing such a seizure, one is struck by the seemingly automated or programmed characteristics of the movements and behavior. Lip smacking, chewing and swallowing motions, various verbal utterances (usually not distinguishable as words), hand rubbing, clapping, and foot stamping are common. The behavior is classically not goal-directed, and there is nearly always total amnesia regarding the episode. Typically, a clearing of the symptoms follows, and the child becomes fully alert and cognizant. These seizures generally last from two to three minutes up to an hour and are usually caused by a lesion in the temporal lobe. One affected child was known to experience psychomotor seizures approximately four times yearly. Within an hour, the relatively normal and typical behavior of the twelve-year-old boy progressed to shredding wallpaper and linens to physically aggressing upon his mother. He experienced a compulsion to run through traffic and break windows.

CASE STUDY V

Teacher's Report (Barbara L., 11 years old, 5th grade)

Barbara has been in the fifth grade for the past four months. It has been noticed that while writing on the chalk board, she appears to lose attentiveness. That is, during a math exercise she may stop in the middle of the project, look at the ceiling or floor, and then resume activity on the board. It was thought she was distracted by other class members. However, further observation revealed that she will perform this bizarre behavior when there are no obvious visual or auditory distractions. Academically, she is doing average work in reading, spelling, and arithmetic. Barbara has been labeled by the other students as a "show-off" because she will periodically fall to the floor from her chair or drop books, pencils, and other objects.

She claims this behavior is not purposeful and during these episodes has been observed to stare off into space for usually less than a minute. Although Barbara relates well to her peers, they sometimes become impatient with her. Many complain they must repeat a conversation because she does not listen. Recently a close friend became angry and stomped away. This close friend related that Barbara was staring at the floor and did not seem to understand one word that was said during the conversation. Barbara is a hyperactive child and it was previously considered that many of the symptoms were a result of this condition. However, as the weeks passed by, it became evident that Barbara is troubled by something other than hyperkinesis.

Alternative Solutions

1. Apply behavior modification techniques to gradually lengthen attention span.
2. Refer her to a neurologist for a suspected petit mal seizure disorder.
3. Observe more carefully the symptoms of inattentiveness, falling to the floor, dropping of objects, and take new baselines on this data.
4. Advise that the parents have her placed on medication to help remediate the hyperactivity/inattentiveness.

Recommended Solution (Barbara C., 11 years old, 5th grade)

Although Barbara is well liked and doing average academic work, she has problems with inattentiveness. These problems occur when she is writing at the chalkboard and conversing within the classroom atmosphere. Furthermore, she has been known to fall to the floor and drop books and other objects. During these occasions she is unaware of her behavior. She has been labeled as a show-off because of the above activities. Some students have become annoyed because she frequently asks them to repeat what they have just told her. The baselines taken by the teacher indicate she is inattentive for less than sixty seconds, and this occurs frequently during the school day.

Alternative 1 suggests gradually lengthening the attention span through the use of behavior modification techniques. Although behavior modification techniques can in many cases lengthen attention span, the other related symptoms such as falling to the floor and dropping objects suggest that the child is experiencing something greater than an attention loss. Because of the related symptoms, it is likely that any attempt at behavior modification will not result in lengthening the attention span.

Alternative 3 suggests that more sophisticated baselines should be taken by the teacher. Although it would be helpful to obtain more detailed baselines, there is enough information within the teacher referral to make some determination of the type of disorder the child is experiencing. Furthermore, in an extremely large class of twenty-five or more students, it would be difficult for a teacher to exact better baselines than those provided.

Alternative 4 suggests that the parents should have the child placed on medication. Stimulants are usually the preferred medication for hyperactive, distractible, and inattentive children. However, it appears this child is not distracted by any overt auditory or visual stimuli. This is exemplified by her activity at the chalkboard. Therefore, to place the child on medication would not be the most suitable alternative.

Alternative 2 suggests that the child should be referred to a neurologist for a suspected petit mal seizure disorder. This is the most likely alternative. The child has many symptoms of a petit mal or absence attack disorder. In the referral data, the teacher should elaborate on the specific symptoms, which include staring off into space for less than sixty seconds from six to twelve times during the school day, falling to the floor, and losing attentiveness while performing at the chalkboard. On all these occasions, the child does not indicate cognitive activity. In the implementation of such a referral, the teacher should be in close contact with the principal and/or behavior specialists.

In most cases of petit mal, the child will be placed on an anticonvulsive medication which should prevent further absence attacks. Since it is not usual for children described as "inattentive" to actually experience absence attacks, this is one of the first symptoms that the teacher should investigate.

MINIMAL BRAIN DYSFUNCTION

With the current interest in learning disabilities, the literature is flooded with references to minimal brain dysfunctions. While school psychologists and mental health professionals use the term freely, it is usually the case that few can define the term accurately or describe the behavioral and neurological characteristics of the condition. A systematic and detailed description of a child's behavior viewed in the context of the following variables is necessary if minimal brain dysfunction is used as a diagnostic category. Educators and psychologists approach the

MBD condition through the framework of academic disabilities and behaviors respectively. Physicians prefer to describe it in physiological and organic terms. Still others view MBD as a perceptual disorder exclusive of emotional and academic parameters.

It is of further importance to distinguish between the terms *minimal brain dysfunction* and *minimal brain damage*. The former refers to subtle behavioral, academic, and perceptual components whose activities fall short of those expected in the so-called normal child. To substitute the word damage for dysfunction adds nothing. It carries negative connotations for many people. The term erroneously implies brain lesions whose existence is questionable, and it is not diagnostic in encouraging remediation or modification of behaviors. The following is a definition for minimal brain dysfunction (Clements, 1966):

This term as a diagnostic and descriptive category refers to children of near average, average, or above average intellectual capacity with certain learning and/or behavioral disabilities ranging from mild to severe, which are associated with deviations of function of the central nervous system. These deviations may manifest themselves by various combinations of impairment in perception, conceptualization, language, memory, and control of attention, impulse or motor function. These aberrations may arise from genetic variations, biochemical irregularities, perinatal brain insults, or other illnesses or injuries sustained during the years critical for the development and maturation of the central nervous system. . . .

The following nine variables are diagnostic components of minimal brain dysfunctions.

Activity Level—Hyper/Hypo

The majority of MBD children display hyperactive behaviors. They cannot sit still for more than a few minutes at a time, and they are frequently labeled by others as problem children in view of excessive energy and inability to follow a teacher's or parent's orders. They are often asked to slow down, to sit straight, to stop talking, and to act like other children. Parents and teachers usually fail to understand that the child can exert only minimal control over his activity level and that this characteristic is one of many difficulties of learning-disabled and perceptually disorganized children. The hyperkinetic child is characterized by verbal and motor overactivity. Motor hyperactivity may be evident by the child's turning, opening, twisting, or bending manipulations of the objects around. Because motor displays of hyperactivity command so much attention, it is seldom realized that the condition may also be sensory in nature. This sensory type of hyperactivity is defined by the child's inability to refrain from reacting to stimuli. The child simply cannot choose from those stimuli which are appropriate and ignore those which are not. In short, behavior is based on stimulus alone. In terms of behavior, the hyperkinetic child may be identified by the following nine generalizations.

1. can sit inactive for only a few minutes,
2. has a short attention span,
3. fidgets,
4. has difficulty following directions,
5. fights with and teases his classmates,
6. talks incessantly,
7. is easily distracted from classroom projects,
8. is in constant motion, and
9. because of the previous eight reasons, is usually a discipline problem.

Burks (1960), in somewhat more technical terminology, adds the characteristics of poor judgment and impulse action, low frustration tolerance and irritability, poor perceptual and conceptual abilities (reflected in serious academic deficiencies), defective memory, and poor muscular coordination. Moreover, Keagn (1971) reports that the child's impulsive behavior seems unaffected by either reasoning or punishment and that the actions are highly unpredictable. Approximately 4 percent of elementary school children are characterized by hyperactivity (Stewart, 1970). Since a large number of hyperactive children suffer from perceptual motor impairments, it is wise for the examiner to formally examine the child's auditory and visual perceptual systems or have them evaluated by an appropriate specialist.

Hypoactivity is much less common in the case of MBD, although it is frequently identifiable in clinical settings. It is characterized by a child with very sluggish and delayed motor movements and may strike the examiner as the direct opposite of a hyperactive youngster. These children have sometimes been confused with such labels as withdrawn, depressed, or absorbed in their own private world. When asked to hurry, they frequently make numerous perceptual mistakes, realize memory deficiencies, and become frustrated with demands that they cannot hurriedly process.

Attention Span

A short or inadequate attention span characterizes most children at some point in their lifetime. In emotional crises or during periods of physiological upset, anyone may realize an inability to attend, resulting in reduced productivity. It is, therefore, important for the teacher to distinguish between the child who has a short-term or inconsistent attention deficit based on situational factors from the child who is consistently unable to sacrifice his concerns and interests by committing a reasonable length of attention to another task.

Therefore, this term should be used as a descriptive statement in diagnosing minimal brain dysfunction only if it is described and identified consistently as typical behavior of the youngster. Parameters of short attention span can be both visual and auditory, that is to say, some children may show either visual or auditory inability to maintain attention. It is, therefore, important for the teacher to be aware that either or both of these conditions may predominate a child's attention deficit.

Distractibility—Stimulus-bound

Closely related to hyperactivity and short attention span is the concept of distractibility in identifying minimal brain dysfunctions among children. It is utilitarian to use the term *stimulus-*

bound, which identifies the child who is unable to refuse attention to any impending stimulation, interchangeably with distractibility. The distractibility can be visual, auditory, or haptic. Distractibility can be external or internal but can be thought of most commonly through examples of noise and visual interruptions. It is important to identify the conditions under which it occurs, its frequency, and the sensory modalities involved. These youngsters are frequently distracted by peripheral movement, classroom noise, visual interruptions, and body functioning. In another context, these children may be described as selective attenders to varieties of coincidental stimuli which conflict with the expected tasks at hand. In the large majority of children, these distractible stimulations have no relevancy to current demands made of them.

Perseveration

Perseveration refers to an individual's inability to terminate a task upon its reasonable completion through internal controls. There are three basic ways in which this behavior occurs. The first, perseveration of motor behavior, is the most common. The child may become engrossed with a physical activity from a game and continue it for the behavior's sake well after its completion by others. Or, another child may perform a pencil and paper task, become engrossed with the movement, and literally write a repetitious activity off the edges of his paper. On a verbal level, a child may become infatuated with a word, be unable to proceed to the next word and continue its repetition after that demand is terminated and another one is introduced. Thirdly, and less commonly perceived by teachers and clinicians, is the perseveration of thought. This is to be distinguished from overproductivity of thought in which repetition of the same stimulus is not a critical feature. Exaggerated repetition of thought content and process, either because it is pleasing to the child or because s/he finds comfort in its redundancy, is the identifiable feature. Some children who perseverate their thought have described the mental imagery and experience of playing with a toy in the same movement, in the same setting, over and over to the point of inappropriate preoccupation. Thought perseveration is less common and more difficult to recognize. It is best identified after a trusting relationship has been cultivated with a child where there is a willingness to describe fantasies, private thoughts, and mental gymnastics that are commonly shared with no one.

Impulsiveness

Impulsivity is another variable which overlaps into descriptions of short attention span, distractibility, and hyperactivity. Still, in pure form, it implies a behavior, instantaneously produced, which the child cannot resist performing. Decision making is seldom deliberate; decisions appear to be characterized by poor judgment, and the child is frequently asked why inappropriate activities were performed. A child's answer is usually, "I don't know," and that, in point of fact, appears to be the truth of the matter. It is suspected that neurological encoding processes may be responsible for such spontaneous and poorly planned behavior, although the research is inconclusive on this issue at the present time. From the teacher's viewpoint, s/he may describe some frequency of behavior in which a child destroys a paper and pencil task with some activity totally unrelated to the assignment. Again without anticipation or planning, a child may junp up from a seat, become engaged in physical activity totally unrelated to the expectations set, and subsequently find confrontation with authority and peer groups. Children sometimes describe the sudden realization of being in an activity of which they had no earlier awareness or recognition.

Affective Fluctuations

The MBD child's emotions are commonly volatile and spontaneous. The child is quick to anger, to experience joy, and to find frustration. Emotions are poorly integrated and are distractible from one to the other. However, it is important to think of this child in terms of the excessive demands that impinging stimulation seems to bring about. Consequently, the emotions are equally disorganized. However, this youngster should not be thought of as aggressive, mean, or uncaring for others. On the contrary, this excessive emotionality is not deliberate, and the child's heart is easily won by those who project accepting and trusting affections. This youngster's cyclothymic mood changes are a direct function of environmental stimulation and are easily distinguishable from psychopathological personality disorders which are often pervasive in nature and difficult to attach to a specific event. A child with such mercurial affect cannot be described routinely and consistently in exclusive terms of emotional illness. Rather, emotional energy is contingent upon the mood of the present environment, the crisis confronting the child, or the joys and frustrations over which there seems no control. Most commonly, the search for a predominant emotion will meet with failure, and one will usually conclude that a mixture of positive and negative emotions is the norm.

Language Disability

Language is defined as an organized system of symbols used by humans to communicate on an abstract level. It may be evaluated by investigation of expressive and receptive communication abilities. The child with MBD characteristically displays language- and symbol-related disorders. These children often distort or substitute connecting words in sentences and manifest peculiarities in sentence structure. It is important for the teacher to become familiar with a child's attempts at language and to look for distortions in the child's communication abilities. In evaluating language disorders, the teacher should concentrate on how well a child understands messages given orally and his/her ability at expressing or encoding information. The inability to comprehend information is not a function of auditory organic impairment but an inability to decode or process information given the child. It is not a result of low intelligence but the child's inability to sort auditory symbols. These children, thus, are experiencing perceptual deficits.

Some children may exhibit a problem recalling a term, the name of an object, or the word they need to complete a sentence. These children will attempt to describe an event or an object in their environment and constantly say "you know what I mean."

"At the fair the other day I saw . . . well, it was on tracks and made noise, it's a, uh, you know what I mean, it was long and had cars and made smoke. . . ." The child was attempting to recall the word "train." Children with these disorders are described in the literature as having dysnomia. Dysnomia is the inability to recall the word one needs in describing an object or event or retrieving information that is necessary to complete the sentence communication.

Children with language disorders will constantly make mistakes in sentence structure. It is important not to over-react to a child who makes one or two mistakes over a long period of time, but the concern is with the child who constantly demonstrates peculiarities of words and word order. Examples of such peculiarities include:

1. "At least I don't stow stones"
2. "I am going to grandmother's house in the bus hound"
3. "I'm selling gerbils for free today"
4. "The Grand Canyon is a little big hole"
5. "I saw a flying bird in the yard back"

Children that are detected as having language disorders should be referred to speech and language specialists. If these professionals are not available within the school system, the school psychologist or guidance counselor should be alerted about the communication disorders. Through early recognition and identification, remediation programs can be established which will further alleviate any potential gross problem as the child goes on in his educational pursuit.

Perceptual Deficiencies

Before determining whether a child is experiencing minimal brain dysfunction with respect to faulty perceptual processes, investigation needs to be made into the visual and auditory sensory modalities. The child must be able to see and hear raw stimuli in which sensation does not necessarily progress into perception. Perception, on the other hand, is the process of organizing and interpreting the raw data obtained through the senses (Lerner, 1971). The child who cannot hear well will have difficulty following directions and thus may show false signs of auditory perceptual deficiencies. Visual deficits may also erroneously resemble an MBD characteristic when the child simply needs glasses to correct a visual error. There have been cases reported where children were evaluated by school psychologists for perceptual deficiencies with recommendations for remediation based on psychological and educational test findings. In the process, the examiner overlooked crucial diagnostic examination of the child's sensory systems. On one occasion, an alert teacher discovered that one of these children could not discriminate colors in different numbers from letters in close written work. After an examination by an optometrist, the child was fitted with glasses, and the alleged perceptual problem vanished. Physical and neurological anomalies of the visual and auditory tracts must be evaluated before attributing the existence of dysfunctions to perceptual deficits. If problems are suspected to be organic in nature, the child should be referred to an ophthalmologist or otologist for visual and auditory screening.

Many characteristics of major organic dysfunctions are similar to the MBD symptomatology. This is particularly pertinent to children with frank or obvious brain pathology such as manifested by convulsive disorders, cerebral palsies, and gross disorders of mentation. In the true MBD, however, the motor and cognitive systems have subtle or less obvious impairments.

Perceptual error reveals itself in visual and auditory nonperipheral impairments. While the sense organ is physically healthy, some central nervous system insult or aberration appears to disrupt encoding or decoding abilities. A youngster may accurately perceive and decode materials while being unable to organize them neurologically and thus respond accurately. In such cases, encoding disturbances are the predominant feature of nonperipheral impairments and are commonly described as perceptual problems. The use of the term *perceptual problem* should be discouraged, as it has come to mean many things to many people and offers little by way of specific description of the MBD child's sensory experience.

After eliminating concern for sensory organic deficits and major dysfunctions, the teacher can assess the perceptual processes by informal methods. S/he may devise ways of checking a child's vision and hearing. The youngster could be asked to perform various tasks to assess discrimination and sensory interpretation. Commands which may be employed to assess such visual skills as recognition, closure, memory, sequential memory, and figure-ground are as follows: copy these letters, match these words and numbers, describe these facial expressions (visual recognition); show me the parts missing from this picture, put this puzzle together, say the word these separate letters form (visual closure); show me the picture that is missing, draw the design from memory (visual memory); write out the letters of the alphabet and numerals from 1 to 12, put the pictures back in sequence (visual sequential memory); pick out the capital and small *r*s in this paragraph, point to all the animals in this scene (visual figure-ground).

Assessment of auditory skills may be made in the same manner: point to the direction of the sound, write the words which I dictate to you as I am walking around the room (auditory localization); close your eyes and identify as many noises as you can hear, tell me the word when I give you part of it—*chool* = school, *ani* = animal (auditory closure); follow three directions —close the door, hand me the book, sit in the chair—in the order given, tell me the story in order (auditory sequential memory); point to the animal this sound represents, tell me the sounds that you hear on the playground which are loud and soft, turn around in your chair and tell me where you begin to hear my voice (auditory localization). If further evaluation is necessary, formal testing by an appropriate specialist is recommended.

Visual disturbances may reveal themselves in reversals of the kind commonly associated with a small child's initial learning attempts. As an MBD characteristic, these children may substitute *d*s for *b*s, *p*s for *q*s, and even *m*s for *w*s. In more extreme form, dysgraphia may be apparent, in which a child displays pervasive inability to produce numbers and letters. This syndrome may be associated with rotations, fragmented symbols, collisions, size alteration, and closure difficulty of individual symbols. Teachers should be encouraged to identify as specifically as possible the reversals that are common or the ways in which the child's dysgraphia is apparent. If encoding and decoding aberrations are suspected, they should be described in the predominant terms of the child's visual or auditory error. While many teachers think of perceptual error in relation to visual and auditory difficulties, a host of additional factors are involved. Probably the most common perceptual error reveals itself in the intense difficulty of some children in learning right from left; they cannot then project that difficulty in discrimination in their own bodies to others and to inanimate physical objects and events around them. It is of little use for parents and teachers to chastise this child for failing to remember, as this faulty behavior is clearly unintentional.

The MBD youngster's poor sense of directionality is a common variable and is also characterized by his inability to distinguish between such forced choices as up and down, before and after, front and back, enter and exit, in and out, AM and PM. They frequently experience orientation deficits in both space and time, and these children are often unable to tell time. They may be unable to accurately perceive yesterday from tomorrow or to coordinate their own bodies in relation to spatial limitations. Impaired body imagery involves difficulty in locating one's own movements in space.

Fine and Gross Motor Disorganization

Among MBD children, both fine and gross motor incoordination is common. However, one may be predominant or exclusive in the child's inability to walk on tiptoes, to hop three yards on one foot, to skip, or to crawl on all fours in a coordinated fashion. In addition, running, climbing, and jumping skills which demand gross or large muscular coordination are often deficient.

In case of fine motor incoordination, the child may have difficulty tying shoes, drawing and writing with pencil and paper, cutting with scissors, and zipping and buttoning clothing. The criterion here involves the performing of movements demanding small muscular coordination. Awkwardness and incoordination typical of the above examples are soft neurological signs (Charlton, 1972).

In addition to fine and gross motor incoordination, many MBD children display associated movements. This condition can be observed in parallel body movement unrelated to the child's activity. Put differently, the child may rhythmically move the tongue or foot in association with an attempt to perform a finger task. These surplus or association movements do not parallel the original intent of the activity which is being performed. Mirror movements are a somewhat classical example of this and are characterized by a child who parallels another body movement with one intended on the lateral side. For example, if a child is asked to touch each finger of the right hand with the right thumb, s/he can be observed to approximate that same movement with the other hand. On a more gross motor level, a child who is having some conversational difficulty may be observed to thrust the shoulders forward in an attempt to aid the communication process. Mirror movements, parallel sequence, and lateral movements are descriptions of the same behavior which is commonly referred to as associated movement. Some children and adolescents exhibit one or many soft neurological signs. On most occasions, the teacher will find that these symptoms are slight and difficult to recognize.

CASE STUDY VI

Teacher's Report (Jay N., 9 years old, 3rd grade)

Jay is described as having serious academic problems but no overt or obvious psychological difficulties. He is alert to his peers, conversational, and friendly. However, he is reading at a primer level and is repeating the third grade. He has difficulty with spelling and is unable to copy materials correctly from books, papers, or from the blackboard. An optometric evaluation earlier in the year revealed normal vision.

His inability to process visual stimuli is indicated by inadequate and incorrect responses to letters, words, and numbers. For instance, reversal and crowding of letters was evident in such tasks as writing his name. Often one letter would collide with others. He reverses individual letters within words. When given copying tasks, Jay does not always progress from left to right. He is left handed and often starts to write in the middle of the line or page. When writing numbers, he begins at the bottom of the page and moves upward. Often the symbols are unclear, and frequently he will leave out a number.

Written and oral sequencing tasks are extremely difficult for Jay. He cannot spell words containing three or four letters after repeated exposure. He cannot repeat the days of the week, seasons or months of the year. He may pronounce "felt" for "left," "was" for "saw," etc. Words phonetically decoded may contain reversals as well as sequential disorder. For instance, when decoding the word "passenger," he may miscall the beginning sound by saying "ab" instead of "pa." His difficulties are further compounded because he demonstrates sequential and reversal disorders in combination. For instance, he may pronounce and write "out" for "not," "dog" for "gob," "ban" for "nap," etc. Further, given a simple cvc (consonant, vowel, consonant) word with the beginning consonant missing as in "ag," he cannot supply a consonant to make a word. He usually moves the final consonant to the initial position ("ga") and then adds an ending consonant to make a word. However, he is able to make a short cvc word when the final consonant is missing.

Jay's history of school failure began in kindergarten. His first- and second-grade teachers gave him a great deal of individual attention. His parents revealed a history of slow development in gross motor skills as well as short attention span, distractibility, and hyperactivity. They did not know what to do about the problems.

Alternative Solutions

1. Recommend the student to the school psychologist for diagnostic testing and possible placement recommendations.
2. Recommend the student to the remedial reading teacher.
3. Recommend the child to the learning strategist.
4. Recommend placement in a special education resource room.

Recommended Solution (Jay N., 9 years old, 3rd grade)

Jay has had a history of educational difficulties. His parents were aware of earlier teacher complaints but were unaware that anything further could be done with him. They noted developmental delays, distractibility, hyperactivity, etc. There were no obvious psychological and social difficulties indicated by the parents or by the third-grade teacher. The strategist and resource room models indicated in alternatives 3 and 4 are mainstreaming concepts for mildly handicapped children. This student appears to have severe learning disabilities. These are indicated by reversals in letters and words, directionality confusion, writing clarity problems, reading and spelling difficulties, phonetic problems, etc. Such problems require a complete educational and perceptual training program, usually found only in a self-contained classroom program. The learning strategist and resource rooms usually cannot devote the time to such severe long-term handicaps. Therefore, these two alternatives are not the most useful.

The remedial reading teacher is concerned primarily with educational tasks related to reading. Thus, option 2 is a less-than-adequate alternative since it treats only a segment of the problem and does not deal with underlying perceptual aspects.

The severity of this child's problems suggested above indicate a need for a diagnostic evaluation by the school psychologist. The most appropriate alternative is option 1. The evaluation should specify the exact disorder as well as provide a detailed remediation program. In such a case, the evaluation might be done in conjunction with a learning disabilities specialist. Subsequently the child may be placed in a self-contained classroom or some other facility which assures more continuous involvement with one concerned professional.

SUGGESTED READINGS

Clements, S. D., Davis, J. S., Goolsby, C. M., and Peters, J. E.: *Physician's Handbook: Screening for MBD.* Little Rock, Arkansas, Ciba Medical Horizons, 1973.

This book was written primarily for physicians but is highly suitable for classroom teachers. It was compiled by educators, psychologists, physicians, social workers, and speech pathologists. This is a highly readable book which provides basic concepts into minimal brain dysfunctions. Essentially the book is divided into the following areas: preschool, elementary, language and psychological screening, special neurological examination, and obtaining background information from parents on family history. The book provides several behavior rating scales and is an excellent resource for obtaining a general overview of minimal brain dysfunctions. Additionally, it provides information on the location of the State Directors of Special Education. Classroom management suggestions are given, along with those management techniques which can be used in a home environment. Suggestions are also given for working with the family, school, and others involved with the young child who is categorized as having minimal brain dysfunction.

McLoughlin, J. A., and Wallace, G.: *Learning Disabilities Concepts and Characteristics.* Columbus, Ohio, Charles E. Merrill, 1975.

Wallace and McLoughlin have compiled one of the most concise and enjoyable books in terms of presenting basic concepts of the child who has learning difficulties. There are several chapters which are of particular interest in understanding the child with learning problems, including concentrations on perception, language, reading, written language, arithmetic, and social and emotional problems. The book also provides information on parental screening and participation in intervention techniques as well as devoting a chapter to the prevention of learning disabilities.

Kirk, S. A., and McCarthy, J. M. (Eds.): *Learning Disabilities Selected ACLD Papers.* Boston, Houghton Mifflin Co., 1975.

This is a book of readings by a number of well-known authors within the field of learning disabilities. Of particular interest is that the selections concentrate on the educational and medical practices and management of children with learning problems, on reading and dyslexia, with a section devoted to adolescents and their problems with learning. Because this book has a variety of articles by different authors, it gives the reader a more global view and understanding of the field of learning disabilities.

Siegel, E.: *The Exceptional Child Grows Up.* New York, E. P. Dutton, 1974.

The book by Siegel concentrates on the exceptional child who has associated brain injury, and it supplies helpful hints for recognizing as well as dealing with these children. It is of particular interest because of the way it concentrates on minimal brain dysfunctions and various combinations of impairments in learning, behavior, language, perception, coordination, personality, and social insight.

Chapter 4

Emotional Assessment

Chapter Objectives

- *Three significant characteristics of disorganized thinking which may be found in the elementary school-age youngster.*
- *The concept of superstitious activity and how it interferes with the psychological and intellectual functioning of children.*
- *Distinguishing between the characteristics of withdrawal and creative fantasy and how each behavior may occur in school-age youngsters.*
- *Definitions of the following symptoms and how an observer can detect them through contact with the child.*
  - *a. delusions*
  - *b. withdrawal*
  - *c. suicidal characteristics*
  - *d. affect disorders*
- *Differentiation between a child who is characterized as having a social perception disorder from one who is deliberately antisocial.*
- *The concept of psychogenic body dysfunctions and the symptoms which characterize this problem in young children.*
- *The reason why it is important to be alerted to the diagnostic indicators of suicide in children younger than nine years of age.*
- *One explanation for the occurrence of phobic reactions in children and two variables which would make a child more susceptible to such a reaction.*
- *The differences between mood and affect.*

A CHILD WHO IS SUFFERING from a number of emotional and behavioral problems cannot learn effectively in the best educational environment. The same is true with a child who has a learning disability. Some children may be of average to above-average intelligence, but due to the learning problems, they cannot learn effectively by traditional teaching. Children beset by emotional problems cannot make maximum use of their educational opportunities. A teacher's facility with informal assessment of emotional dynamics is necessary because this skill facilitates the identification of psychological disorders which may not otherwise be recognized.

When a child experiences an educational deficit, it is important that the teacher identify the problem as specifically as possible. This is essential for appropriate testing and subsequent remediation by a mental health specialist. Similarly, when a child suffers from an emotional disorder, it must be assessed before remediation. It is the purpose of this chapter to identify a number of symptoms and characteristics which are suggestive of psychological problems. The psychological symptoms presented here range from typical mild to severe disorders.

It is not unusual to find a child who shows heightened anxiety while anticipating an examination or a competitive athletic event. Situationally determined symptoms as a rule are not as serious as those which are persistent and occur frequently under most situations. A child who constantly shows sluggish motor movements, lacks affective responses, speaks in a monotone, and complains of unhappiness for no apparent reason must be considered for a psychological evaluation and therapy. Referral to a mental health specialist should occur when the child experiences several symptoms, either similar or dissimilar, and when these symptoms are of moderate to severe intensity. Additionally, referral should be implemented when the teacher needs more information about the child's personality dynamics in order to relate more effectively. The emotional evaluation area of this chapter is divided into five major sections:

1. Disorganized thinking
2. Display of coping mechanisms
3. Conflict and anxiety
4. Psychogenic body dysfunctions
5. Social and self-perceptions

The reader is not required to follow each section in sequence but may choose to move from one area to another in order to gain familiarity with informal techniques for evaluating emotional behavior.

DISORGANIZED THINKING

Disorganized thought is based on three major characteristics: lack of orientation, delusional ideation, and sensory distortions. It is always essential to determine a child's contact with reality and the process by means of which new information is assimilated into the personality structure. Determination of orientation in three spheres (time, place, and person) and assessment of delusional thought and altered sensory experiences will help identify adjustment needs. Children are sometimes known to ramble irrationally in verbal content and in the expression of thought. In such cases, there is usually confusion in separation of the real from the unreal and in the youngster's own perceptions of self in relation to the real world.

Orientation

A youngster may exhibit confusion of *time* and lack awareness of its influence on daily life. This variable can be partly determined by asking the child to identify the date, complete with the day of the week, month, and year. Psychotic children or children with gross reality loss may have no awareness of this information and be locked into their own private world of time sequence.

Children's description of their fantasy in relation to time, place, and person will usually identify the degree to which the time factor has lost its meaning. A fifth-grade, ten-year-old child who constantly confuses mornings with afternoons, days of the week, months, seasons, and/or lives in a year that has not arrived is experiencing time disorientation. Appropriate adjustments for the child's age and intelligence must be made when more advanced comprehension of time is lacking.

Clinical experience with children has indicated that orientation to *place* is less crucial than that of time and person in view of a child's already limited understanding of the surrounding world. In any case, it is important to understand the child's sense of directionality and to determine the degree of comprehension about the immediate environment and the familiarity with which the child moves. In fugue states (states where brief lapses of consciousness occur with no recollection), it is not uncommon for children to lack orientation to place and to be unable to describe the position in which their home, school, and neighborhood environment fits into a cognitive map structure. Such children may have difficulty moving from place to place and sometimes are heard to ask seemingly senseless questions about where they are and how they got there. At other times, expressions of confusion and statements about orientation in one or more spheres may follow sudden awareness that things are very disordered. The child who is uncertain as to his own identity, who adopts the character of another, and who does not respond when his name is called, probably experiences disorientation of *person*. Severe disorders of person are discussed under the next major topic area, delusional ideations. However, the major concern is the child who shows extensive disorientation in any one or more of the three areas mentioned.

The child suffering from lack of orientation will show confusion in other areas of thought. Thinking, for example, may be illogical and lack coherency. Such children may be suffering from a more severe disorder, perhaps of a psychotic nature. These children become confused, tend to ramble illogically, and show preoccupation with their own internalized thinking; their written work will lack organization and will demonstrate little resemblance to the required assignment.

There are children, on the other hand, who have not learned proper orientation behavior because of cultural differences. They have not been exposed to time and place orientations. However, they should have awareness as to who they are. These children must not be confused with those suffering from emotional disorder, and the symptoms may be quite similar. The difference is that children with an emotional disorder will usually show symptoms of inconsistency, confusion, and illogical thinking in most, perhaps all, areas of thought expression.

The teacher must also be able to identify the child with a severe language disorder which can cause difficulty with time, place, and person orientation, although not to the same degree as with emotional disturbance. The language-disordered child can be taught proper orientation, but the emotionally disordered youngster will not make changes with typical educational approaches. Another distinction is that the language-disordered child will not manifest extensive thinking difficulties, confusion, and consistent illogical thought expression. Naturally, as the child grows older, s/he is expected to become more oriented in the three spheres. Some children under six years of age are not typically oriented in time, place, and person because they have not developmentally reached the level of understanding that is expected of older children.

Delusional Ideation

Delusions are false beliefs. In more extreme form, orientation in person may assume bizarre qualities of reference ideas in which a child believes that he has taken on the body and character of another individual. Classical psychoanalytic literature is a good source for familiarizing the reader with delusions of identity (Arieti, 1955; Freud, 1959; Jung, 1936). The more common display of this phenomenon occurs in individuals who have excessive preoccupation with a personality character and who attempt to assume that person's behavior. A child may identify with Superman. There are recorded instances of youngsters trying to fly from buildings wearing Superman costumes. Another youngster may assume the characteristics of a Biblical character and attempt to cleanse souls and achieve some ideal perfection. Still other youngsters may identify in less pathological form with athletes, movie actors, and relatives in which their own identity is confused with that of the other character. These cases are less dramatic, and psychological intervention can usually correct such marginal delusions of character quite easily if they are identified in early stages of development.

Other common delusions among children center upon hypochondriasis, grandeur, and persecution reactions. The hypochondriacal concern about body function usually takes the form of the child looking for somatic symptoms that resemble a disease. It is not unusual for a parent of these children to be excessively concerned about physical health. The child learns such reactions, and they become bonded into the personality. A slight sore throat may be magnified with the preoccupation of having the tonsils removed.

If a youngster adopts the character of another individual for the purpose of elevating his own worth, delusions of grandeur may be present. Grandiosity is characterized by assuming the qualities of another individual which are judged to be better than one's own. If, on the other hand, a child adopts the character of an individual which invites abuse and criticism from others, there is said to be delusions of persecution.

Classical examples of this thought disorganization occur in individuals who believe that they are Jesus Christ or a canonized saint who is persecuted by heathens and nonbelievers. Again, the payoff for such beliefs is in cleansing guilt and achieving perfection through ideations of reference in others. Children experiencing severe delusions are easily noticed by their peers and are often teased. Teachers can become alerted to severe delusions during routine conversations with the child. Such children are in need of professional assistance if the delusion is preoccupying their thought processes and if they are tending to act on the demands of their false beliefs.

Sensory Distortion

Sensory distortions or hallucinations are false perceptions of sensation in the various sensory modalities. Most commonly, hallucinations occur in the auditory form, in which an individual experiences imaginary voices without the physical presence of another person. Auditory sensory distortion may take the form of one's name being called or may occur in a persecutory nature, in which voices forecast the individual's doom, the likely occurrence of death, or that the individual will be haunted and/or pursued by someone. When asking children if they hear imaginary voices, it is usually important to be sure that the child understands the question since many children respond "yes" in reference to dream experiences and other common imaginary games that children play. Occasionally a professional psychologist may be told that imaginary voices are heard when further questions reveal that nightmare or dream activity is the reference from which the question is being answered. It is, therefore, important that the child understand the question to mean, "Do you hear voices as clearly as you hear mine when you are awake and when no one is around?" This usually serves to offer a child a reasonable method with which to distinguish true hallucinations from common and normal imaginary experiences. Children have sometimes been observed to suddenly change facial expression, to glance quickly over a shoulder, and to generally exhibit the characteristics of an individual being summoned by a voice. When auditory hallucinations do occur, they are often identifiable by such sudden and overt changes in movement and facial quality.

Visual hallucinations are less common but may occur in severely disturbed children. In one case, a child had been abused as a youngster and passed from foster home to foster home numerous times. He had also witnessed violence on several occasions and eventually had extreme difficulty sleeping because of the bloody faces that he viewed nightly in his bedroom window. This particular child also experienced auditory hallucinations in which he heard voices of victims and cries of pain immediately outside his bedroom. In another case, a child watched a ball of modeling clay and described the process in which a devil's face began to take shape and bleed. This particular youngster also commonly looked outside the psychologist's office to an attic window across the street and described the movement of monsters and devils inside the room. In many nonpsychotic youngsters, hallucinations appear to occur when the child is experiencing extreme stress. Such hallucinatory phenomena tend to vanish when the stress is absent. Hallucinations approach psychotic proportions when the child begins to follow the dictates of the sensory distortions and is unable to clearly delineate reality.

It is relatively uncommon for hallucinations to occur in other sensory modalities. However, it is sometimes the case that children experience tactile or kinesthetic sensations of a distorted nature. Such youngsters might describe insects crawling about their bodies or relate the experience of electrical impulses pulsating on the surface of their skin. Other youngsters may imagine that skin tissue is rotting away and describe the feelings that are experienced in the process. It should always be remembered that hallucinations are experienced as *real* and that imagined sensation and perception in any sensory modality is as marked as the real experiences of any other child. Hallucinations are relatively easy to identify, even in the child who intently denies that there are any deviations in sensory experiences. The denial usually opens the door for further questioning in a nonthreatening way which should then be responded to appropriately. It is primarily this area of the informal assessment that will help determine the degree of children's contact with reality and the extent to which they are appropriately oriented and realistically anchored in their environment.

It is through this section on thought organization that the teacher may better understand children's thinking and make some determination of the appropriateness of their cognitive flow. If reality loss is found, the teacher should refer the child to the school mental health specialist. A helpful referral should point out specifically where the reality loss is manifested. If the loss is in the area of sensory changes or ideas of reference, specific attention needs to be made with respect to hallucinations and delusions. Such children may be candidates for placement in special education where they can benefit from the skills of a specialized teacher of emotionally disturbed children. The mental health specialist subsequently will determine the need for counseling, depending on the intensity of the problem after distortion and exaggeration are identified.

CASE STUDY VII
Teacher's Report (Perry K., 10 years old, 3rd grade)

Perry is repeating the third grade at Washington Elementary School. (Washington School is located in a rural area without ready access to special education facilities and school mental health specialists.) Mrs. Salmon, his teacher, chooses to describe Perry's behavior to colleagues as "wierd." She reports that he is particularly difficult to communicate with because he will rarely look at her when she is speaking. Frequently this behavior occurs with other student members of the class. Communication is further complicated due to Perry's very limited vocabulary and his reluctance to respond when spoken to directly. Perry is seldom expressive with any form of emotion, even when it is otherwise apparent that he is either very happy or quite angry.

He regularly practices two behaviors: on occasion, he hits on his own thigh or shoulder, and at times on the playground, he screams out, seemingly at some unseen object across the street from the school yard. Following the screaming, he will begin talking to himself but will stop when other children come within his vicinity. He performs the hitting routine on the average of five times per week, usually in the afternoons, and the activity consists each time of six hits. The screaming mostly follows within the next half hour and consists of a short but loud screech. The conversation following the screams ranges from two minutes to about ten minutes in duration if not terminated by another individual.

Mrs. Salmon recalls that Perry is uninterested in playing with other children in the room, but she has assumed that this may be because he is a year older than the others. He spends most of his free time with his favorite colorful learning aids from the math and science kits. By this time in the school year, Mrs. Salmon feels very frustrated about helping Perry socialize with his classmates. Although he has exhibited these behaviors all year, he is doing average work in all of his academic subjects and will probably successfully complete the third grade.

Alternative Solutions

1. Leave the child alone because he will most likely "grow out" of his symptoms.
2. Attempt to reinforce appropriate behaviors and use extinction for the maladaptive responses.
3. Inform the parents of the specific behaviors and seek their opinions concerning professional assistance.
4. Request the child be placed in a smaller third-grade class where he can receive more individual attention.

Recommended Solution (Perry K., 10 years old, 3rd grade)

It is not unusual to find children with significant learning problems who live in small rural school districts. Many of these districts are without special education and mental health facilities. Consequently, teachers are left with a more difficult problem concerning children with learning and behavioral disorders.

Perry has been described by his teacher as not maintaining eye contact, having a limited vocabulary, expressing very little emotion, inappropriately screaming out to objects or events that only he can see while on the playground, hitting and talking to himself, and not socializing with other children. The teacher indicated further that due to his repeating the third grade, he probably does not have interest in children that are a year younger than himself. Despite these difficulties he is doing average academic work, and it is the feeling of his teacher that he will successfully complete the third grade.

Although alternative 1 suggests that the child may "grow out" of his symptoms, it is unlikely that this will occur. Due to the intensity and frequency of the maladaptive behavior, further investigation of the problem is necessary. Alternative 2 suggests to reinforce appropriate behavior and to use extinction on inappropriate responses. It would be beneficial for his teacher to list all of the inappropriate behaviors and implement a modification program aimed at extinguishing the responses and reinforcing appropriate behaviors that are incompatible with the maladaptive responses. However, such a program requires detailed and frequent contact with the child on a periodic basis. Thus, alternative 2 should be tried by the teacher but only if she has appropriate background in the area of behavior modification and feels comfortable with the system. This alternative, however, is not the total answer to the child's problem. Alternative 3 is the most likely. The parents definitely should be informed about the specific behavior problems and be requested to seek professional assistance. The professional assistance will have to be sought outside of the school system, probably through a local mental health center or private practitioner in psychology and psychiatry. Some of these behaviors may be extinguished by use of a behavior modification system as indicated in alternative 2, but because of the intensity and extent of these symptoms, additional professional services are needed. Alternative 4 is reasonable in conjunction with alternatives 2 and/or 3 since in a smaller class, the teacher could spend more time with the child on an individual basis. However, there are many variables to consider before taking such action. These include the social trauma on Perry by having him placed in another class as well as the feelings of the teacher in the smaller class regarding dealing with his behavior problems. Such a move should only be done in conjunction with the advice of a mental specialist.

DISPLAY OF COPING MECHANISMS

Observable behaviors of children adjusting to the environment will provide the teacher with valuable information about learners' psychological status. This section introduces six variables which are used to evaluate how a child adjusts to changing surroundings: (1) dealing with *stress* and level of *frustration tolerance;* (2) *withdrawal* tendencies; (3) development of *temper* control; (4) degree of *superstitious activity;* (5) consistency of *mood;* (6) nature of *affect.*

Stress and Frustration Tolerance

Children's frustration tolerance is an indication of how appropriately they manage anger and hostility. Youngsters who cannot handle alterations in their routine at home and school or ordinary confrontations with others are likely to display insecurity and instability. Low frustration tolerance usually indicates an inability to effect resolution to stress, in which case excessive use of defensive behaviors often results. One child may experience frustration with an inability to grasp long-division math concepts and appropriately attack that difficulty by asking for the teacher's help or by doing the assigned homework faithfully. Such a child has the resilience to deal with the normal disappointments in the immediate environment and thus eliminate stress resulting from prolonged conflict. Another child may be continually frustrated with losing in games of competition and consequently raise an angry voice at the opponents, throw playing equipment about, and accuse others of cheating. Habituation to this kind of behavior, if stressful, invites ostracism from others and further reduces a child's potential for healthy solutions to disappointment. The same child who reacts with anger at losing a game may project hostility about the surroundings and upon others. This child can be verbally abusive and may even physically aggress upon an opponent. Other children are known to internalize their hostility when angry; consequently they may experience palmar sweating, visceral tension, headache, or other somaticized discomfort. Still other children may react with passive hostility and use strategically placed comments with double meanings for the sake of aggressing indirectly to manipulate the feelings of others.

Withdrawal

Maladaptive withdrawal is characterized by seclusiveness, detachment, sensitivity, shyness, timidity, and a general inability to form close interpersonal relationships (American Psychiatric Association, 1968). Psychological withdrawal is a form of personality constriction with associated characteristics of lack of responsiveness, apathy, and bland affect. Withdrawn children protect themselves from being noticed by refusing to interact with others. Withdrawal is a common maladaptive mechanism for coping with threat.

One child who refused to talk to her kindergarten class received considerable secondary satisfaction by having all her needs met by the other children. Few demands were placed on her, she conveniently escaped much of her school work, and pampering by others reinforced this infantile behavior. In the particular case of this kindergarten child, she spoke freely at home, and there was no underlying organic defect or psychopathology in psychotic dimensions. In treatment, it is critical in this kind of case to remove all of the secondary reinforcers attached to the lack of responding and to make treats, favors, and freedoms contingent upon more responsive behavior.

Excessive withdrawal may be an indication of a functional inability to sort reality. Withdrawal provides an escape into one's own private world which may be designed free of stress and threat. Particularly where inconsistent parental acceptance and discipline have existed in extreme form during the early years, youngsters may create their own world of playthings and friends. Such children are in total control of that world, are free to modify anything which displeases them, and can obtain comfort in escape to their inner sanctuary at almost any time. The teacher is reminded that, by the very nature of withdrawal characteristics, it becomes conflicting and frustrating for children to establish healthy relationships with others (Jenkins, 1970).

Upon being asked, "What three people would you take with you to live on a desert island," one withdrawn child commented, "Me, myself, and I." Other withdrawn children have responded to this question with imaginary playmates or with animated characters of their own creation. The child who demonstrates relatively sudden withdrawal, whether of a physical or psychological form, is likely suffering from intense emotional turmoil. It is essential to determine the extrinsic factors as well as the personality variables contributing to the withdrawal tendencies. Note should be taken of the length of time the child exhibited such a reaction as well as any associated depressive features. These features may manifest themselves in lack of appetite, slowed motor movements, lack of interest, crying, and anxiety.

Temper Control

Display of temper is a variable closely associated with a child's frustration tolerance. Loss of control is frequently observed when a child throws a tantrum or becomes enraged over a relatively minor disappointment. The behavioral display of loss of temper control is often manifested by impulsiveness and is usually accompanied by lack of forethought. A child may even be remorseful for the scene which has been created by a spontaneous loss of control and the failure to anticipate the consequences of these irrational actions. Young children may throw themselves on the floor and gather as much attention by kicking and shouting as they can manage. The teacher who pampers and reinforces this behavior can expect it to continue. The teacher who calmly walks away from such a child is likely to extinguish the behavior.

Tantrums are displays of anger in which the child is attempting to shape the reactions of those in the immediate surroundings. Continuous whining, screaming, crying, or other utterances are manifestations of tantrums. In some instances, they may be associated with excessive motor activity. The classical example of tantrum behavior and its extinction is found in a concise study of Williams (1959). This investigation detailed the elimination of "tyrant-like tantrum" behavior in a young male child who was characterized by prolonged crying prior to going to sleep.

Rage is more common to older children, who lash out verbally and physically when control is lost. It is characterized by a violent display of temper, and it is sometimes followed by amnesia about the event. Rage borders on physical violence, and there is always the possibility that continued rage behavior may result in injury to others or destruction of surroundings. Rage behavior is often accompanied by an individual's desire to be more assertive. The failure to achieve that goal may create continually greater emotional tension, with eventual release resulting in direct physical abuse on the immediate surroundings. Handled properly, the child's loss of control can be less and less satisfying, with a subsequent reduced need for release of these pent-up emotions.

Overcontrol of temper is much less common in children and can be characterized by the child who is "tied up in knots" and seemingly ready to explode. This child has apparently learned that any direct release of emotion is prohibited and knows of no appropriate way to displace the felt discomfort or vent the felt anger. After a prolonged period of such overcontrol, a child may break down in tears, may slip into marked depression, and may plead for help from those around. The child who overcontrols commonly displays psychophysiological symptoms (head- and stomach aches), since this is another method by which children internalize their anxiety and discomfort.

Determining a child's display of coping mechanisms is essential to knowing the level of stability and the capacity for dealing with future stress. The child who resolves conflict appropriately is easily differentiated from one who displaces his aggression overtly. The introverted and withdrawn child is also easily distinguishable from the youngster who gets appropriate reinforcement for social initiative. Similarly, tantrum and rage behavior is easily identifiable and sets the child apart from others who readily adjust to disappointment. Hostility and anger are fairly common among children, and a teacher's experience in identifying this behavior will lead to easier recognition, especially when compared with the normal child's methods of expressing disappointment.

Superstitious Activity

By carefully observing the child in class activity or during a one-to-one contact, the teacher can identify sustained and/or ritualistic motor movements, usually associated with superstitious activity. These behaviors occur in children through a learning process and usually result from a faulty association of events which have occurred in their young lives.

To illustrate, Sullivan's (1953) "parataxic mode of experiencing" fits the model appropriately. The hungry dog, he describes, searches the backyard for food and momentarily stops to urinate. While lifting his leg, someone throws a bone over a nearby fence and the dog quickly runs to the bone and proceeds to devour it. When hungry for food on other occasions, the dog may lift his leg as if to urinate. Through anthropomorphism, it can be assumed that the animal associated leg lifting with the finding of a bone. Similarly, by accidental learning, superstitious behavior may be exhibited by a child who will eat only a certain breakfast food because he believes it will help him perform better on spelling tests. From an earlier experience, he learned an association between the breakfast food and a high grade on a spelling test. Other children have been known to open imaginary doors on their foreheads in order to allow the teacher's lecture to be absorbed. Still another youngster put T-shirts on backwards prior to a competitive game of ice hockey. Some children have been known to search for hours for four-leaf clovers because when one was in their possession on another occasion, they performed very well in a ballgame.

Sustained motor movements such as touching a finger to the thumb and/or head movements may be superstitious behaviors. They are so labeled because they do not facilitate or enhance the performance of a child; they are excessive or surplus movements that are purposely performed. Superstitious behavior is inappropriate when children are unaware of it and when they perceive a direct relationship between their activity and prior events. It is pathological when the behavior interferes with ongoing responsibilities. If a child must go through a series of superstitious rituals to prepare for an activity and inadvertently delays his or her performance, the behavior is maladaptive. For example, one child made the sign of the cross so many times prior to entering the batter's box in a baseball game that the game was delayed. This activity also generated anxiety and impaired his batting potential, as indicated by his consistently striking out!

Perhaps the best indication of superstitious behavior in pathological proportions is the generalization of the rituals to other areas. The child may perform a ritual before eating breakfast, taking a test, participating in an athletic event, urinating, and going to bed. In such cases, a child's movement can soon be completely bound up and at the mercy of inappropriate activities. An emphatic belief that the generalized rituals have a direct causal effect on efficiency should be taken as an indication of adjustment difficulty.

Mood

Mood changes usually involve ambivalence, constriction, inappropriate emotional responsiveness, and loss of empathy for others (American Psychiatric Association, 1968). This behavior is often characterized by withdrawal, regression, and disturbed thought processes. While the more common disorder of mood is revealed in depressive states, a severe alteration in mood may take the form of euphoria, elation, and mania. If a mood disorder takes psychotic proportions, it is specifically responsible for whatever loss of contact the individual has with the personal environment. Some disorders of mood are directly related to a precipitating event, and such depression may exist in either psychotic or neurotic dimensions.

A precipitating event is any identifiable attribute, event, or stimulus which produces or triggers a significant change in mood. Failing a test, being humiliated by another child, losing in a competitive game, developing a physical anomaly, or forgetting to complete an assignment are examples of precipitating events which may produce depressed mood states in elementary school-age children. In other cases, there is no clear precipitating life experience accounting for the pathology of mood. Major mood disorders may take the form of manic-depressive states, with either elation or depression the dominant feature. In some cases, mood swings are so common that they may occur within a relatively short period of time. If there is no clear evidence of an insult on reality, then mood swings are probably anxiety-based through unresolved conflict. Children have been known to remain depressed for months over the loss of a close family member or teacher or over an unexpected divorce of parents. In the latter example, a youngster may be in severe conflict without any recognizable way of alleviating the upset and hurt feelings. Depression has been known to follow the loss of a pet, the birth of a sibling, a move to another city or residence, a failing grade on a test, and concern for world affairs or the plight of starving people in other countries.

Mania as a disorder of mood is much less common in children and must be distinguished from hyperkinesis or behavior disorders stemming from brain injury. In children, a manic disorder is almost always associated with swings toward depression and is often recognizable by either the child or the parent's description of extremes in mood. Some parents and teachers learn to predict such mood swings in youngsters. The child is usually quite perplexed by the reasons for such extreme changes in mood. One child vacillated between moods of depression and elation without precipitating stress. This youngster usually pursued physical activity to the point of exhaustion followed by crying himself to sleep and remaining depressed for several days at a time. His mood swings were cyclical, and another episode of intense and exhaustive physical activity could be expected every two or three months. The child was clearly not hyperactive, nor had there been any overt insult to the brain which might account for mood swings of an organically based nature. This child differed from the hyperactive youngster in his extreme behavioral changes. The hyperactive child, in classical form, remains stimulus-bound and can predictably be expected to constantly maul his environment. S/he may respond to environmental management, while the child with a disorder of mood usually will not. Mood swings in children are almost always learned, although it is wise to assess any evidence of head trauma as an event precipitating extremes in behavior. Should mood swings constantly interfere with the child's school performance, playground activities, and peer relationships, then s/he is a likely candidate for a referral to the school mental health specialist.

Affect

Recently, educators have become interested in affective development; they are already witnessing confusion as to the difference between affect and mood. In an article entitled "Affect, Mood, Emotion, and Feeling: Semantic Considerations," Ketal (1975) elaborates on definition problems and attempts to clarify the situation by explaining the differences between affect and mood. Mood and affect are not synonymous. They reflect different psychological features even though they are both felt (symptoms) and expressed (signs) emotions. Affect implies spontaneous and immediate feeling; it reflects happiness, pleasure, sensation, and thought through verbal and nonverbal body language. Mood implies a stable, consistent, and less flexible emotional state that is not subject to spontaneous and variable fluctuations. Display of affect refers to the observed expression of emotion such as happiness, anger, elation, etc. The self-report of emotion is referred to as affective sensations. The feelings of emotions are not always visible by others, and consequently the term *affective sensations* is used to identify internal feelings.

A child's display of affect or emotions should be routinely observed in a classroom atmosphere. One can distinguish between light affect—that displayed by a child with a happy-go-lucky smile who relates to the teacher with ease—and flat or dull affect—that characterized by the child who never smiles, who speaks only when spoken to, and whose interpersonal social skills appear somewhat arrested. Children are less careful about wearing façades during examinations and interviews than are adults, and their display of affect is usually real and observable. A friendly and affable child may be curious about the classroom and may spontaneously begin conversation about friends and peers. This child appears happy, pleased with the surroundings, and interested in sharing time with others. One can use the terms light, happy, friendly, smiling, sociable, spontaneous, and conflict-free in describing healthy affect. On the other hand, the teacher can use the terms blunted, dull, flat, labored, and unresponsive in describing an unhealthy display of emotion.

Assessment of coping mechanisms helps the teacher to make some determination of how children are adjusting to their surroundings and the degree of reality contact. Typically, children characterized by low stress and frustration tolerance and frequent temper outbursts are candidates for counseling. Prolonged depression, sustained superstitious behavior, withdrawal, and inappropriate affect can all be indications that the child is troubled and that professional help is needed.

CONFLICT AND ANXIETY

Children who are facing major dilemmas that they cannot resolve are suffering from a conflict situation. Conflict usually results in anxiety which stems from threat or anger. Unsuccessful attempts to resolve the conflict may result in heightened anxiety. While all children suffer emotional conflict in their growing years, most adjust appropriately and realize remissions of symptoms in reasonable time. Others develop emotional disturbance from a traumatic incident and become pervasively anxious, ridden with unresolved conflict, and depressed because of a felt inability to make upsets go away.

English and English (1958) define conflict as "the simultaneous functioning of opposing or mutually exclusive impulses, desires, or tendencies; or the state of a person when opposed impulses or responses have been activated." The opposing forces are of approximately equal strength, which makes a choice between alternatives all the more laborious. A conflict situation in the life of a child may be illustrated by the teacher's order to perform an aversive act coupled with a threat of punishment if the act is not accomplished. Conflict is apparent in approach-approach, approach-avoidance, or avoidance-avoidance dichotomies (Lewin, 1935). Examples will illustrate the basic framework within which each kind of conflict operates.

Approach-avoidance conflict is perhaps the most common variety and is expressed by a child's desire to pursue a behavior on the one hand and the fear or anxiety to allow it on the other. A boy may wish to walk down the street to play with a favorite friend but may experience avoidance in knowing that a large dog that has previously attacked him must be met on the way. Avoidance-avoidance conflict is characterized by forced choice of two almost equally undesirable alternatives. A diabetic girl may resist daily insulin injections but face elevated blood sugars and the realistic threat of acidosis as a consequence. In this case, she can at best avoid only one alternative and is necessarily forced to live with the consequences of the other. Approach-approach conflict is a more desirable forced choice for most children in which two attractive alternatives are placed before a child. A boy may be torn between choosing to attend a Saturday baseball game with his father or spending the weekend on his grandparents' farm. Again, only one choice can be made, with conflict generated by his inability to participate in both activities.

Anxiety may be defined as a fearful and unpleasant emotional state in which continuing effort to gain comfort seems likely to miss its goal (English and English, 1958). The source of anxiety may be clear, as in a particular child's failing efforts to master the multiplication tables, or it may be pervasive, in which a youngster experiences a feeling or threat without knowing what is threatening. The former, in which a clearly identified source exists, may be thought of as objective anxiety. The latter, pervasive anxiety from unknown sources, is relatively easy to identify but more difficult to treat. A pervasively anxious child will be clearly unable to describe the original causes of the discomfort. This condition constitutes the inherent problem for a mental health specialist in remediation—identifying sources before any effort at desensitization can be made. A third-grade girl who fidgets, squirms, twists and tugs at her hair, wrings her hands and taps her fingers, sits on the edge of her chair, and projects fear and uncertainty in her surroundings, is obviously anxious. The experienced teacher will learn to observe nervous mannerisms and will acquire skills for making fine discriminations between various quantitative and qualitative levels of anxiety.

Trauma

A trauma is defined as an upsetting experience which results in conflict and anxiety reactions (Harriman, 1965). Trauma depends upon perception of the event. The death of a first-grade teacher may have a powerful impact upon a child but result in little feeling among others in the community. A youngster who loses a turtle on the school playground may experience trauma and anxiety while searching for the small animal. Much of children's ability to handle stress resulting from trauma depends upon their past experiences. If children have had gradual exposure to more intensive traumatic situations, their resistance may be high; however, if trauma is too intense and too frequent, their resistance is naturally diminished (Denenberg and Bell, 1960; Gauron, 1964).

A youngster may be traumatized by an incident of violence directed at one of the family members, by being attacked by a large animal, by being sexually abused, or even by being convinced about being wicked. Traumatic experiences of children include finding a favorite babysitter dead on the front lawn, witnessing a drunken father nearly fulfilling his threat to murder the mother, and being suddenly faced with a Santa Claus costume at a very tender age.

Residuals of traumatic incidents most often involve approach-avoidance conflict in which a child would like to indulge in one pleasurable activity but has difficulty doing so because of an avoidance tendency inherent in the choice. Upon invitation from her alcoholic father, a young girl may relish the possibility of a trip to an amusement park but suffer severe avoidance conflict because of a recent traumatic physical abuse incidence perpetrated by the father on such an occasion. Another boy may long to go on a nature hunt with the school class but choose to stay home because of a phobic fear of snakes stemming from an incident where an older boy threw a dead snake around his neck.

Sexual Expression

Many children harbor conflict and anxiety in relation to sexual expression. A child's conceptualization of personal sexuality is sometimes an index of feelings of self-worth and importance. If the child has learned an appreciation of personal sexual identity in the family, if nudity, with modesty, has been considered acceptable in the home, and if frank and digestible answers to questions involving sex are given, the child is likely to have few problems in psychosexual development. The child who is chastised for exploring the genitalia, for failing to be fully clothed, or for attempting to satisfy natural sexual curiosity with questions is likely to misunderstand sexual feelings and identity. The disturbed child may be obsessed with body functions, with clandestine masturbation, or with incessant verbal expression of otherwise normal sexual concerns.

During the first three years of his life, one little boy was exposed to excessive sexual intimacies between his mother and her common-law husband. At age three, the youngster was removed from the home, experiencing virtual obsession with sexual functions. He was later known to make crude attempts to copulate with pictures of nude females from pulp magazines and to approach foster brothers and sisters for extensive sex play. He preferred to talk about sexual behavior in all conversation with both children and adults and often paged through magazines in hopes of finding pictures of sexually stimulating females. At the tender age of five, he had initiated homosexual contacts with foster brothers, could describe oral-genital sexual behavior in detail, and attempted to recreate many of the scenes he had witnessed between his mother and common-law stepfather. It was over a period of many months that these concerns were gradually desensitized, placed in proper perspective, and understood as expressions of adult sexuality. It was important to approach his preoccupations and interests in total frankness with suggestions for curbing his own behaviors through substitution of healthy interpersonal activities in his new family. By contrast, the healthy child would be expected to be curious about sexuality but not to become so preoccupied with the subject that it interferes with gaining satisfaction from other pursuits.

While psychoanalytic theories of psychosexual development have questionable validity for some mental health professionals, theory does offer terminology and framework within which to understand childhood identity development. In his original framework, Freud (1949) identified oral, anal, phallic, and genital stages of psychosexual development. Understood in behavioral terms, his descriptions do encourage analysis of the child's early years in terms of his sucking, biting, elimination, and genital exploration behaviors. The youngster's home life and its atmosphere will in part determine health or pathology of the child's sexual expression and role identification. Parents should allow small children of the opposite sex to bathe together and should view sexual exploration and curiosity as normal developmental behavior.

There are many theoretical frameworks for understanding psychosexual development which can sharpen the skills of the diagnostic interviewer for recognizing pathology in the child's early development (Erikson, 1963; Horney, 1937; Sullivan, 1953).

Fantasy

All children commonly daydream about fulfillment of their wishes, and it is often a fine line between such normal expressions and pathological fantasy in excess. Unfortunately, withdrawn children who typically escape into their own private worlds are often allowed to remain in the back of the classroom relatively unnoticed by teachers because they do not attract anyone's attention or cause trouble. However, it may be this very child who finds the world painful and who consequently designs personal parameters of reality to make life more tolerable. Axline's *DIBS in Search of Self* (1964) and Greenberg's *I Never Promised You a Rose Garden* (1964) are both excellent descriptions of the private worlds of emotionally disturbed children who have found fantasy more attractive than reality. Healthy fantasy may include wish for ownership of a material object that a child is unable to purchase, or it may involve plans for helping the family live more comfortably together. In his spare time, a boy may daydream about a bicycle, about his father taking him hunting or fishing, or about earning good grades in school and pleasing his parents. A distinction between healthy and unhealthy daydreaming is the child's inability to terminate fantasy trips. Excessive frequency and duration of such indulgence may also indicate pathology.

Hutt and Gibby (1959) provide a useful distinction between creative and withdrawal fantasy. In either case, fantasy is an attempt to create more comfortable living conditions than presently exist. If a child uses fantasy in a creative fashion to plan, organize, and change an environment and improve personal living conditions or those of others, then the ambitions are basically healthy. If, on the other hand, a child's fantasy life is created for the sole purpose of escaping discomfort, then fragile reality testing in a world viewed as unchangeable is encouraged. In other words, the child is encouraged and challenged to test fantasized beliefs against real-life situations. When the teacher or parents report that they never know what a child is thinking, that s/he seems to be constantly in a dream world, talks excessively to self, and does not use the opportunity to play with other children, then one can suspect fantasy withdrawal. Conversely, if children are creative thinkers, pursue their ideas, and are independent and ambitious, then creative fantasy is being practiced.

Some children indulge in very vivid fantasy. Such fantasy may be so detailed that the child includes names for imaginary characters, experiences withdrawal under stress, and lacks interest in normal surroundings. The child may float in and out of fantasy for an hour or more. This kind of withdrawal fantasy suggests that the child is in need of psychological intervention. It is not uncommon for teachers to notice that a child is indulging in excessive fantasy or daydreaming. Some of these children have been known to interact with fantasized playmates and carry on conversations with them. However, this should be differentiated from the normal occurrence of imaginary playmates in young children. The child becomes a candidate for treatment when the fantasies are prolonged and preferred routinely over play with the peer group.

Phobic Reactions

A phobic reaction is an uncontrollable and irrational fear of an object or situation. (Anxiety, it will be remembered, is the expectation of anticipated danger and is usually aroused by numerous stimuli.) Some phobic reactions, such as fear of the dark and of being left alone, have a tendency to decrease with age and experience. Phobias are learned and stem from tangible sources such as animals, objects, or places. Intangible sources of fear are not considered phobic and are more accurately labeled anxiety resulting from anticipation of danger or threat. As the child grows older, fears change from tangible to less tangible stimuli. Most two-year-old children are fearful of loud noises, while six-year-olds are not. The latter are inclined to fear more imaginary experiences.

Eysenck and Rachman (1965) point out that there are several variables which may influence anxiety reactions. These same factors apply to phobias, since irrational fears contain an anxiety component. These variables include the following: (1) personality factors or the predisposition of the child's nervous system to learn anxiety reactions, (2) degree of confinement (physical and psychological restriction of the child), (3) intensity of the unconditioned stimulus (strength of that stimulus which evokes the anxiety reaction), (4) age (the largest number of fears occur with younger children), (5) past experiences (fears are reduced when the child has been introduced to them gradually), and (6) type of conflict (approach-avoidance producing the greatest anxiety). The tense child who is exposed to a shouting teacher will acquire a school phobia much quicker than the child who is gradually introduced to similar noxious stimuli when relaxed and in a state of confidence.

Feared objects or situations have a tendency to generalize to other closely related stimuli. A classical example is given by John Watson, the founder of Behaviorism, who taught an eleven-month-old child to fear a white rat and then generalized the fear to other similar objects. School phobia often generalizes but is originally a learned reaction from a localized anxiety, with the focal point being an irrational fear of attending school (Levinson, 1962). It is common to find children with school phobias who fear teachers, students, and other stimuli closely related to the school environment (Kelly, 1973). The fear usually begins with one experience such as embarrassment following the child's inability to write his or her name. It may also be triggered by a major stimulus such as a death within the family (Tietz, 1970).

Basically there are two kinds of school phobic reactions, Type I and Type II. The Type I child comes from cooperative parents and a psychologically healthy (in most areas) home where there is adequate communication and parents readily achieve an understanding of school-phobic dynamics. The onset is usually the first episode, and the child makes a rapid response to therapeutic intervention. Treatment can relate directly to the symptom—fear of school. However, a Type II child has uncooperative parents, tends to be older, and does not rapidly respond to therapeutic intervention. This type is serious and difficult to remediate; the child may require hospitalization. The onset is incipient, and poor communication between parents exists. Mothers tend to show neurotic reactions, and fathers typically have character disorders. A Type II child experiences a dual tragedy—family turmoil and school phobia. By introspection, Type II disorders will demand modification of the home atmosphere and specific treatment for the school phobia. A summary of the two school phobic types is given in Table V.

TABLE V

CHARACTERISTICS OF TYPES I AND II SCHOOL PHOBICS

Type I	*Type II*
1. The present illness is the first episode.	1. Second, third, or fourth episode.
2. Monday onset, following an illness the previous Thursday or Friday.	2. Monday onset following minor illness not a prevalent antecedent.
3. An acute onset.	3. Incipient onset.
4. Expressed concern about death.	4. Death theme not present.
5. Mother's physical health in question; actually ill or child thinks so.	5. Health of mother not an issue.
6. Good communication between parents.	6. Poor communication between parents.
7. Mother and father well adjusted in most areas.	7. Mother shows neurotic behavior; father, a character disorder.
8. Father competitive with mother in household management.	8. Father shows little interest in household or children.
9. Parents achieve understanding of dynamics easily.	9. Parents very difficult to work with.

From Miller, L., Barrett, C., and Hampe, E., Phobias of childhood in a pre-scientific era. In Davids, A. (Ed.): *Child Personality & Psychopathology* 1974, pp. 89-134. Courtesy of John Wiley & Sons, Inc., New York.

Moreover, uncontrolled environmental circumstances produce phobic reactions. After being placed in bed for the evening, a seven-year-old child was frightened by the wind current slamming his bedroom door closed. The child learns to fear small rooms, dark places, and being left alone. Children with phobic reactions are candidates for a desensitization therapy program which gradually introduces them to the feared situation. Any attempt to force the school-phobic child to attend school without professional therapy can result in greater anxiety and increased fears.

Suicidal Characteristics

Suicide results from very severe conflict and is closely associated with despondency. It may be examined from a commit and attempt perspective. A suicide commit is any deliberate act of self-damage which results in death, while attempted suicide is nonfatal (Stengel, 1972). Suicide statistics for children under five years of age are largely unknown, and rates for children between five and nine years of age are extremely low (Schuyler, 1973). The methods of attempted suicides for children under eight years of age include jumping from windows, dashing in front of automobiles, jumping into rivers, turning on household gas jets, and ingesting poison (Bakwin, 1957).

Although childhood suicides are rare occurrences, the threat of suicide is more frequent. Children may ruminate about such an event in an effort to get back at a teacher, a peer, or a member of the family. Adolescent suicide in the United States has been on the rise, especially for those above fourteen years of age. While adolescent females make more attempts, the suicide commit rate among their male counterparts is higher. The lower success rate in females could be the result of their choice of method, which is less violent than that used by males. Females utilize poisons and drugs, whereas males employ guns and strangulation. Since the view of death in young children is incompletely developed, any gesture or rumination of suicide should be considered dangerous.

Three states of children's concepts of death have been identified by Nagy (1959): (1) Children under five deny death and usually view it as a separation which is temporary and reversible. (2) Children between the ages of five and nine years imagine death as a second person and are able to identify with those who are already deceased. Children at this age acknowledge death but for the most part keep it averted from themselves. (3) Beyond nine years of age, children begin to realize the meaning of death as cessation of bodily activities which is inevitable and could affect them. Because of their incomplete view of death, all suicidal references should be considered serious. The child may be the victim of suicide while only intending to alarm and manipulate selected others.

Children who talk of suicide often experience private suicidal ruminations. In some situations, suicidal attempts are a deliberate means of focusing attention on unfulfilled needs. Children experiencing suicidal thoughts usually demonstrate other personality problems such as depression, low ego strength, and feelings of inadequacy. When children are overwhelmed by such negative emotions, it is difficult for them to sustain proper performance in academic tasks. Whether the child threatens or attempts suicide, it should be explored with proper seriousness. Common suicidal signs to look for in children between the ages of seven and eighteen have been identified by Mattsson (1969) and include such behavior changes as withdrawal, lack of interest, loneliness, crying, diminished appetite, and sleep disturbances. External pressures such as family turmoil, loss of a loved one, and poor academic performance may potentiate suicide. The teacher should not be hesitant to ask direct questions when suicidal thoughts are suspected and make appropriate referral. Questions may include (1) Have you ever tried to hurt yourself, and (2) Have you ever wished you were dead?

CASE STUDY VIII

Teacher's Report (Tom F., 11 years old, 5th grade)

Tom will soon be entering the sixth grade at Stuart Elementary School. He is the third of four boys, and his parents are divorced. Tom currently resides with his maternal grandparents. He is a likeable, friendly, and conversational youngster who is in no apparent physical distress. However, he has a rich fantasy life and has been known to adopt wild stories as realistic events in which he was personally involved. He told several peers recently that his father was on special assignment to the President of the United States and that his mother was acting as his secretary. Further, he related that he had special bionic powers which he would only use in emergency situations. Not only did he relate this kind of information to his peers, but he frequently writes about it during composition. In fact, he will write about such topics when he should be writing about a book or other assigned events. Another teacher remarked that while in the second grade he tended to be disobedient, disorganized, irresponsible, and preoccupied. Academically, he has been doing poorly in all his subjects although it is felt that he is intellectually capable of doing much better. His peers are beginning to react to him by withdrawing, teasing, and name calling. He is becoming upset by their reactions, but he is not reducing the quantity or quality of the bizarre stories he creates and shares.

Alternative Solutions

1. Refer the child to the school psychologist and relate the aforementioned symptoms.
2. Obtain more precise information as to behavior disorders and academic deficiencies.
3. Request that the child repeat the fifth grade.
4. Obtain a detailed history of the family background and status of the current divorce situation.

Recommended Solution (Tom F., 11 years old, 5th grade)

According to the teacher's report, Tom has been experiencing a number of psychological as well as educational handicaps. Apparently these handicaps have existed for a number of years. The main core of these handicaps centers around a fantasy life of relating wild stories as realistic events, preoccupation, and rejection from his peers. Although his teachers feel that he is capable of performing well in an academic setting, it seems as though psychological conflicts are suppressing his academic abilities. To request that the child, as indicated in option 3, repeat the fifth grade is inappropriate because no attempt is made to relieve him of the psychological conflicts that could be affecting his academic performance. In all likelihood, by having the child repeat the fifth grade, he would experience the same psychological conflicts, since there is an indication that these have existed over a long period of time.

Option 4 is also rejected. In this case, it would not be as important for the teacher to obtain current information on the divorce status and family background. Although this information may be helpful in an evaluation of the child, it could be accomplished by one of the school social workers or mental health specialists. If the teacher knows of reliable information in this area which may be useful in the diagnostic evaluation of the child, the data should be passed on to the school psychologist.

Option 2 is particularly unreasonable. Although there is fairly precise information available regarding the behavior disorder which this child is experiencing, his academic deficiencies could be defined more precisely. That is, information should be given on each academic subject concerning Tom's current status.

Option number 1 is obviously the most appropriate. The child will need a thorough psychological and perhaps educational evaluation and probably will need counseling. It seems likely in this case that the psychological conflicts and symptoms are suppressing the child's academic performance. Thus, with counseling, many of the symptoms will be relieved, and the child will show improved performance.

PSYCHOGENIC BODY DYSFUNCTIONS

When physical symptoms stem from nonorganic causes, they are identified variously as functional, psychosomatic, psychophysiological, and psychogenic. Common psychogenic disorders include enuresis, encopresis, stomachache, headache, and sleep disturbances. Functional symptoms often confuse teachers, parents, and physicians who are inclined to consider somatic disorders organic in nature. If the child successfully uses psychogenic physical complaints to avoid responsibilities, this behavior becomes reinforced and is likely to be used with increasing frequency. This phenomenon is referred to as secondary gain. The major disturbances discussed below are not meant to be comprehensive but are the more common psychogenic symptoms in children. There are three guidelines mental health specialists follow in determining functionally based physiological disorder: (1) the child's prior use of physical symptoms as a means of avoiding activity, (2) the presence of sufficient emotional stress precipitating somatic symptoms and (3) evidence that the symptom is used to solve a conflict under stress.

Guidelines for Determining Functionally
Based Physiological Disorders

1. Child's prior use of physical symptoms as a means of avoiding some activity.
2. Presence of sufficient emotional stress.
3. Evidence that the symptom is used to solve conflict.

Figure 2

Enuresis

It is not uncommon for preschool, kindergarten, and first-grade children to wet their clothing. Outwardly, many of these children do not appear to be suffering from internal conflicts. After appropriate physical examination and negative findings, personality assessment will begin to uncover underlying anxieties. By the very fact that these children realize that others are aware of their problem, they develop a low opinion of themselves.

Enuresis (involuntary discharge of urine) can occur at night (nocturnal) or during the day (diurnal). Diurnal bladder control is usually obtained by the third year of life and prior to nocturnal control (Homan, 1969; Hurlock, 1968). When a child stops diurnal wetting, it is a good indication that nocturnal enuresis will terminate within the next year. Moreover, when a child begins to demonstrate discontinuous nocturnal wetting, bladder control is nearly complete.

For therapeutic and diagnostic purposes, mental health specialists divide enuresis into three major categories: organic, chronic, and regressive. Organic enuresis refers to the presence of an underlying physical etiology. It is estimated that between 5 and 10 percent of children experience enuresis because of medical problems such as bladder infections, diabetes, epilepsy, or genitourinary anomalies (Finch, 1960; Pierce, 1967). In addition, many children who maintain their wetting problems do so because of deep sleep disturbances and therefore do not gain necessary wakefulness (Pierce et al., 1961). Chronic enuresis means that the child has never obtained bladder control. Children with a chronic disorder often have one or more close blood relatives who were enuretic. Although these children may go to bed at night with good intentions of waking to urinate, they invariably discover that they have unknowingly wet their beds. Parents of chronic enuretics will confirm how difficult it is to wake their child at night. There are numerous cases where children suffering with chronic enuresis have continued to exhibit the symptoms up to fifteen years of age. Most frequently, the young adolescent blames himself for lack of bladder control and suffers from severe feelings of inadequacy. This low self-esteem is further heightened by the historical nature of the enuresis.

Regressive enuresis refers to the child's loss of bladder control once it has been obtained. The child who has been dry and begins to wet because of some psychological stress is characterized by regressive enuresis. Such pressures as the birth of a sibling, school failure, high parental expectations, and movement of the family to a different location can be causative factors. Spontaneous remission may occur once the child has adjusted to a new situation.

In some instances, counseling is beneficial, especially if the child asks for symptom relief or displays other emotional signals under stress. Once the teacher has discovered diurnal enuresis, it is important to know the precipitating factors, if any and to refer the child to the school mental health specialist.

Encopresis

Encopresis is involuntary discharge of feces. Encopretic children soil their clothing during the waking hours and occasionally while sleeping. Many will state that they did not feel any urge to go to the toilet. With occasional lapses, most children obtain bowel management around two years of age, and it normally occurs prior to bladder control (Hurlock, 1968). Allowing additional time for developmental lags, it is a fair estimation that children should have good bowel control by age three. As with enuresis, some children have never acquired bowel control while others have and later regressed.

Encopretic children are frequently inhibited and embarrassed following the occurrence of the fecal mass. There is a strong tendency for them to avoid activities which call for close interaction with peers. On the other hand, there are some children who are not noticeably affected by encopresis and who will continue playing with their friends after learning that they have soiled themselves. More often, these youngsters have problems with adults who may persistently scold them about poor toilet habits. Although the literature is sparse concerning the causal factors of encopresis, it is generally viewed as originating from a developmental failure or from psychological stresses (Garrand and Richmond, 1952; Pinkerton, 1958). Developmental failures result in continuous soiling from infancy, with learning control of sphincter muscles being incomplete. As a result of persistent parental pressures, these children may show negativism and rebelliousness toward authority figures.

Children who soil due to psychological problems may be emotionally disturbed. It is not infrequent for some encopretic children to hide their underwear or change clothing so that they will not have to face embarrassment from their parents, peers, or teachers. In referring the child, it is essential the teacher make note of the frequency and the approximate time of day of its occurrence.

Somatic Complaints

Functional disorders of a somatic nature also include headaches, stomachaches, physical fatigue, allergies, urticaria, asthma, and sleep disturbances. These conditions result from or are aggravated by psychological causes. Once a youngster successfully uses physical symptoms to circumvent annoying activities, these symptoms become reinforced, and the child gradually uses them more frequently. There are numerous school-related activities which a child may wish to escape such as athletic events, examinations, giving reports, and doing specific assignments. Some children can willfully produce such physical symptoms as violent vomiting in an effort to avoid an aversive responsibility.

Headaches in young children are not usually functional (learned or used as an escape mechanism) in nature as they often are with older children and adolescents. Consequently, children of less than six years of age who complain of persistent headaches should have medical attention. Older children and adolescents often experience symptoms of headache because of anxiety and tension (Friedman and Harms, 1967). When a child complains of frequent tension headaches, it is not uncommon to find one or both parents afflicted by the same complaints, thus suggesting that the symptom is learned. Headaches are of concern when the child persistently complains of discomfort and when the pain interferes with ongoing efficiency. It is important to know the time and frequency of occurrence and the psychological factors that contribute to the symptoms.

Stomachache is the most common physical complaint among children. Stomachaches may stem from a variety of conditions and be influenced by family and eating customs. Many children will develop stomachache as a reaction to school pressure or from failure to perform up to personal or parental expectations. Investigation into eating habits may also identify stomach aggravation. One youngster was known to eat breakfast each day before school at a fast-food stand and subsequently complained of visceral pain throughout the day. If a child realizes secondary gain and avoidance of responsibility from the complaints, then symptoms are likely to remain and resist modification. Since children often lack the insight necessary to mention stomachache as a problem related to their emotional condition, mental health specialists routinely explore the possibility that such symptoms can stem from medical anomalies, dietary condition, emotional stress, and malingering characteristics. When the teacher becomes alerted to such conditions, referral should be accompanied by the following variables: time of onset, severity, frequency, and other influential factors.

Hives are a skin reaction of the upper dermis appearing as a wheal and bright red flare accompanied by extreme itching. They are generally considered a result of allergic reactions. Hives are medically referred to as *urticaria* and have been known to result from an organic predisposition which is aggravated by emotional factors. Sources such as heat, foods, and inhalants have been identified as capable of producing urticarial symptoms. Children are especially susceptible to hives under stress.

Another common allergic reaction in children is asthma. Boys are affected twice as frequently as girls prior to adolescence. In most cases, the onset occurs between three and seven years of age. As with urticaria, asthmatic reactions result from many causal factors ranging from foods, molds, and inhalants to emotional involvement. Children can experience asthma during strenuous activity, and it may result from moderate psychological stress. Emotional etiology of asthma may occur when the child is anticipating an upsetting event or when s/he is unhappy and trying to avoid an aversive situation. When possible, the teacher should identify the situational or chronic stresses that precipitate the asthmatic reaction. It is interesting to note that children do not seem to be as annoyed by asthmatic conditions as are teachers and parents. However, the reactions do prevent the child from fully participating in activities and thus may limit involvement, learning, and enjoyment.

The child who frequently complains of fatigue and who sleeps periodically during the day may be using sleep as an avoidance mechanism. These children may claim to tire easily and complain of weakness in their shoulders, neck, and legs. They may sleep in class and appear withdrawn and listless. As with urticaria and asthma, the child who sleeps excessively should have a thorough physical examination before an attempt is made to remediate the symptoms through psychological efforts.

SOCIAL AND SELF-PERCEPTION

Social and self-perception is an area in the affective domain that concentrates on the interaction of children with themselves and others in their surroundings. The concern here is the relationship with other significant individuals such as peers, siblings, parents, and teachers. Included in social and self-perception are the children's perception of themselves (ego strength, body image, confidence levels) and their ability to relate to the environment.

Interpersonal Relationships

Typical social problems to observe in school-age children involve aggression, lying, attention seeking, jealousy, persistent tattling, and teasing. Some of these behaviors are voluntarily expressed by a child and are intended to be negative. On the other hand, some negative behaviors are manifested by children who are not appropriately interpreting social cues. These children show deficiencies in monitoring and forming adequate social and behavioral changes. For instance, the boy who constantly touches his classmates may not understand the verbal and nonverbal cues expressed by others who are requesting him to stop emitting the annoying behaviors. Meanwhile, the other students develop negative expectations of him and he begins to live by their prophecy. With a disorder of social perception, the child persistently commits the same offensive behavior. Tattling to the teacher, talking and laughing inappropriately, and inability to interest others are behaviors exemplified by children with social perception problems. These youngsters will often be saddened and perplexed by reactions from peers and yet be unaware of how to behave differently.

Social perception is defined as the ability to identify and recognize the meaning and significance of the behavior of others.

Sometimes children with social perception problems are categorized as having nonverbal learning disabilities. These children find it difficult to recognize and identify the feelings of others. Ernest Siegel (1974) indicates that when an individual talks, the words themselves account for only 7 percent of what is communicated; 38 percent is conveyed in the manner of speaking, such as with voice inflections and intonations, and 55 percent by facial expressions and nonverbal body language. Thus, the child who has problems interpreting and understanding nonverbal cues has difficulty making appropriate responses to social situations. The child with a social perception problem has difficulty understanding and interpreting the intentions of his fellow classmates. These children may, for example, not interpret nonverbal gestures adequately that they are touching other children too much, tattling to the teacher too often, or saying inappropriate things. Because of this inability to make use of nonverbal feedback the child consistently makes the same social mistakes. Social misperceivers become perplexed and confused as to why the other children do not accept them, and they do not have the necessary insight into themselves to make appropriate alternations in behavior. Doreen Kronick (1972) says that "we do not joke at a funeral or awaken people to impart trivial information; we do not tell an off color story in a streetcar, classroom, or church; we do not involve the supermarket clerk in a deep political discussion as we check out our groceries." The child with social misperception may attempt any of the above.

Children with social perception problems are frequently and mistakenly identified as being emotionally disturbed. However, the basic problem is their inability to interpret the intentions and motives of others. These children need to be recognized by teachers before a remediation can be implemented. Should the child continue to make the same social misperceptions, this will result in a poor self-concept and feelings of worthlessness and inadequacy. These children need individual attention, a thorough educational and psychological evaluation, and a subsequent remediation program to help them establish better social insight.

Such children are distinguished from youngsters with antiso-

cial behavior by four different characteristics. Antisocial youngsters are deliberate with both intentions and behavior. They understand the consequences, experience little guilt, and have a
tendency to lie as well as cast blame on other individuals. Children with social misperceptions, on the other hand, misinterpret
the motives, intentions, and feelings of others. They lack alternatives in approaching others and become perplexed and confused regarding their reactions. The social misperceiver often
experiences remorse, sadness, and despondency. Summary characteristics of anti-social and social misperception difficulties are
as follows.

Antisocial	*Social misperception*
1. deliberate	1. misinterprets
2. understands consequences	2. lack alternatives
3. experiences little guilt	3. perplexed
4. lies—casts blame	4. remorseful

Examples of behaviors which are most likely social misperceptions include a child who teases or makes light of another
child's physical impairment—"Look at Jimmy! He runs funny
because his leg won't work right." Another child may accuse a
classmate of being "dumb" because the student is quiet and re-
served, unwilling to be expressive in the classroom and on the
playground. The social misperceiver may bother the quiet student about the introverted behavior without considering the shy
child's position. An elementary school boy may innocently insist
that girls be involved in very physical, aggressive games which
girls generally avoid, the girl misperceiver may get her feelings
hurt when boys refuse to "play dolls" and assume the role of a
baby or the mother.

Social misperceptions are expressed when youngsters fail to interpret the feelings of others, as when a child regularly brings
up issues that are hurtful to others, i.e. how important fathers
are to a fatherless peer or how bad drinking is to a child with an
alcoholic parent. Talking with one's mouth full, making excessive noise, using unusual physical contact, interrupting, failing
to listen attentively, carrying practical jokes to excess, and ex-

treme attention-getting measures are examples of behaviors that might represent demonstrations of social misperception as opposed to antisocial acts.

CASE STUDY IX

Teacher's Report (Sally S., 12 years old, 6th grade)

Over the past three weeks, Sally's teachers have become increasingly aware that she has withdrawn from other children and has been slow in completing routine assignments. In fact, in several instances she spent a full hour completing a math assignment which, in the past, would have taken her one fourth of the time. On one spelling assignment, she produced so many pictures and scribbles that it was difficult to find the assigned words. She refuses to participate in social activities with her classmates during recess and will not cooperate in projects for small groups in the classroom. During one situation she folded her arms and kept her eyes averted from the others in her group and spoke in a voice that was barely audible.

Sally reported to the school nurse last week that she was always tired and complained of fatigue in her shoulders and neck. She claims that these symptoms appeared during the last week and that she has never had them previously. In the months prior to the last three weeks, she was quick to pursue assignments, was popular with her classmates, and engaged in activities energetically. When questioned, her parents were most cooperative and indicated no major changes in the home environment, but they were quick to add that they have been preoccupied by the illness of their youngest son and have not had the normal time to care for Sally's needs. A recent physical examination does not suggest any physical problems.

Alternative Solutions

1. Observe the child for a longer period of time to see if her problems are resolved.
2. Proceed with immediate counseling sessions and inquire about the trauma or events which may have precipitated the personality changes.
3. Suggest that the other sixth-grade class members help Sally with her problems by giving her more attention and showing greater interest.
4. Suggest to Sally that she stop this nonsense and get back to her old self.

Recommended Solution (Sally S., 12 years old, 6th grade)

Alternative 1 may be a waste of time because the problem has become worse during the past three weeks. With more observation and no intervention, it seems likely that the symptoms will become intensified or remain the same.

Alternative 3 would have only helped Sally become more aware of her "different behavior," the other children may, in effect, actually facilitate her withdrawal. Furthermore, it is difficult for sixth-grade children to understand deficits of their peers, thus Sally could not be helped a great deal by them.

To suggest to Sally, as in option 4, that this behavior is nonsense and request her to get back to her old self is obviously inappropriate. From the onset of these problems, there is no indication that Sally is purposely producing her symptoms.

Alternative 2 is the most correct. Counseling sessions aimed at helping her to become more involved with herself and others are appropriate. Since the withdrawal, lack of conversation, slowness in completing assignments, and physical complaints occurred recently, it is suspected that a trauma at home or at school precipitated the symptoms. When symptoms occur suddenly, the key factor in any cause should be to suspect a trauma. Counseling by the school mental health specialist should readily reveal the difficulty.

There are children who have pulled the head off of their favorite turtle, poked out the eyes of their very own puppy, and pulled the tail off the classroom mouse. Some of these children manifest bizarre behavior through imitation of television violence. These acts do not necessarily identify emotional disturbances but may illustrate faulty social perception processes. The teacher should note whether these experiences are purposeful, antisocial, or the result of social deficiencies. The antisocial youngster is deliberate, understands the consequences of his behavior, experiences little guilt, and knows full well that pulling the head off the turtle results in its death. The child with a social perception deficiency is more likely to harm the turtle, then be perplexed with the outcome and even try to put the head back on.

It is important that the teacher as well as the school mental health specialist (counselor or school psychologist) be able to

SOCIAL PERCEPTION PROBLEMS

(The Case of the Turtle)

Antisocial	*Faulty Perception*
1. Deliberate	1. Misinterprets
2. Understands consequences	2. Lacks alternatives
3. Experiences little guilt	3. Perplexed
4. Lies – casts blame	4. Remorseful

Figure 3

distinguish the antisocial youngster from the one who has faulty social perception, particularly because of the uniqueness of helpful remediation programs. Of significance is the fact that the child with faulty social perception, on most occasions, can be handled quite easily within the classroom environment. On the other hand, the child who is antisocial may be receiving an abundance of reinforcement and reward for undesirable behavior and thus will intentionally maintain a pattern of disruptive acts within the classroom environment. Since children with social misperception simply lack alternatives and frequently misinterpret the intentions and motives of others, the prognosis for positive participation in the classroom is excellent.

Self-Concept and Body Image

Self-concept refers to the child's thoughts about his physical, cognitive, and emotional capacities. The child perceives himself or herself on a continuum as adequate or inadequate. Occasionally, adequacy feelings vary according to situational stresses; thus, an entirely consistent level of self-concept is unlikely.

Children perceive external reality based upon past experiences. Perception of social relationships and expected actions of other individuals depends upon the outcomes of similar historical events (Elkind, 1971). The self-concept influences continuing behavior and is altered and modified by events as they are experienced. These experiences may be satisfying and reinforce positive feelings about the self or they may be dissatisfying and result in negative feelings with future expectations of failure. External stimuli may alter a child's self-perception and result in anxiety. For example, a child may work math problems confidently at the desk setting but become tense and shaky when performing the same activity on the chalkboard.

Self-concept may be altered in a variety of situations, with one of the major influences affecting elementary school-age children being academic performance. Research indicates that children with low scholastic achievement tend to have poor self-concepts and heightened anxiety (Coopersmith, 1960; Hill and Sarason, 1966). Further evidence suggests that academic underachievement in bright male children is directly related to deficiencies in their self-concept. It is not uncommon for these youngsters to perceive themselves as being rejected, criticized, and constricted by others (Walsh, 1956). Elementary children who experience external threat from peers and teachers may also react with poor academic performance. When children are placed in rejecting and threatening social surroundings, their behavior demonstrates irrationality, inappropriateness, and altered self-perceptions.

The following is a set of questions designed to better understand the child's social and self-perceptions.*

1. If you were going away to live on a desert island and you would only take three people with you, whom would you take?
2. What do you especially like to do with your father (mother, brothers, and sisters)?
3. Think of your best friend. What do you do together and why is he(she) your best friend?
4. Think of someone you don't like. What don't you like about him(her)?
5. What kind of animal would you like to be? Why?
6. How do you feel about school? Your teacher?
7. If you could make three wishes, what would they be?
8. Think of a time when you were happy. What was it like; what did you do?
   a. Angry (mad)
   b. Afraid (scared)
   c. Sad (unhappy)
9. If you could be different from the way you are, how would you want to change yourself?
10. How would your mother like you to be different?
11. How would your father like you to be different?
12. Do you feel that you are as smart as other students in your class?

Teachers have more impact on children than is ordinarily realized. One study indicated that negative interpersonal experiences with teachers are more severe and long lasting than such experiences with any other group of individuals, including parents (Branan, 1972).

Body image is closely related to a youngster's self-concept. Perception of one's physical body is influenced by information pro-

---

* Wichita Guidance Center: Interview Form for Children. Unpublished.

vided to a child by significant others. If the frail boy has been teased by his brothers and sisters, he is encouraged to develop a warped and inadequate body image. His warped perceptions become internalized and generalized when he is teased by peers. Reinforcement is intensified when he realizes in actual comparison that he is smaller and weaker than his friends. Self-awareness of differences may cause body image distortions. The girl who has a large birthmark on her leg may not want to take showers after physical education for fear others may ridicule her. Inadequate body image may be manifested by withdrawal behavior in competitive games, and it is always associated with a poor self-concept. Inability to participate in competitive games due to lack of coordination may also have a detrimental effect upon body image.

SUGGESTED READINGS

Davison, G. C., and Neale, J. M.: *Abnormal Psychology An Experimental Clinical Approach.* New York, John Wiley & Sons, Inc., 1974.

This book is of particular importance in understanding the psychological composition of unhealthy behaviors. It approaches abnormal behavior in terms of learning theory, and emphasis is placed on the etiology and causation of variant behavioral patterns. The text is of particular interest because it gives many informal assessments and in-depth techniques for identifying and recognizing deviant behavioral patterns.

Price, R. H.: *Abnormal Behavior: Perspectives in Conflict.* New York, Holt, Rinehart & Winston, Inc., 1972.

This is one of the few abnormal psychology textbooks which offers an overview of the various perspectives on deviant behavior. These perspectives include the psychoanalytic, illness model, learning theory, moral, humanistic, and social viewpoints. It contains numerous clinical viewpoints into variant behavior and is an excellent resource for gaining a thorough understanding of the controversies within the mental health field.

Gordon, S., and Williams, G. J.: *Clinical Child Psychology: Cur-*

rent Practices and Future Perspectives. New York, Behavioral Publications, 1974.

This is a book of readings by a number of well-known authors in the area of mental health. Of particular interest in this book is the section entitled "Advances in Education," which emphasizes the affective dimension of a child's personality. Included are such topics as emotional education in the classroom, health and the education of the socially disadvantaged, and developing and understanding of self and others. This book is recommended for the teacher who wants to gain a comprehensive understanding of the emotional aspects of the child within the classroom atmosphere.

Dupont, H.: *Educating Emotionally Disturbed Children.* Readings, 2nd ed. New York, Holt, Rinehart & Winston, Inc., 1975.

The book by Henry Dupont is a useful resource for the identification, classification, diagnosis, and planning for children with emotional problems within the elementary classroom. Additionally, emphasis is placed on the recognition of problem behaviors in the regular classroom, the resource room, the special class, the managing and modifying of classroom and academic behavior, etc. It is totally oriented to the educational environment and provides techniques and methods for the remediation of emotionally disturbed youngsters.

Conclusion

WITHIN MANY PRIVATE HOMES, most classrooms, and every school, there are children who are experiencing unusual difficulty with the normal learning process because of exceptionalities in their growth and development. Too few people who have regular contact with these youngsters are in possession of the basic diagnostic assessment information and skills which assure reasonably accurate identification of these troubling disorders. The result is simply that an unbelievable number of children are prevented from enjoying the greatest potential available through the formal education process. The enormous potential of formal schooling will be realized more and more as parents, teachers, and mental health specialists become aware of the contributions each is able to make to the others, especially in regard to the identification of the innocent children whose educational progress is hampered by various physical and psychological deficits.

This text has introduced information about common learning problems of young children so that interested persons can make two important contributions: (1) adjust their own relationship with a child beset with a difficulty, and (2) make an intelligent, helpful referral of a troubled child to a qualified professional. The information contained in this text is especially designed to be as nontechnical in language as possible without oversimplifying or misrepresenting symptoms and disorders. The reader is cautioned to study the descriptive language carefully so that premature and inaccurate conclusions about children's behaviors are reduced. However, the authors are convinced that one who has considered the elaborations about exceptional behaviors contained here and has a suspicion that a child may be troubled will be well advised to prepare a referral that is based on the less technical descriptions in this text.

The basic conviction of the authors is that all children want

133

to achieve, perform well, adjust, and be recognized for excellence. The authors are thus committed to the notion that almost all children who experience unusual deficits in growth and development are children who are beset with subtle influences over which they have little control unless identified. This commitment leads to the issuing of a challenge to those who work with young learners to become better equipped with skills which lead to proper identification of problematic behavior. The information supplied here serves as a basis for such skill development and deserves to be thoughtfully internalized.

Finally, if the point has not been satisfactorily made, a more active interchange of information, observations, and evaluations among the various persons who are involved with children is sincerely encouraged. Parents ought to share information that is unique to the home environment. Teachers must be more active inquirers with mental health specialists as well as with parents. This level of inquiry involves both searching for answers and giving the information that can only be gleaned in a classroom setting. Mental health specialists have an obligation to be accessible to teachers and parents so that basic information that is associated with their expertise is delineated (1) in response to questions about particular cases, (2) through seminar/workshop settings, and (3) in planned practicum-type associations with parents and/or teachers. Reducing communication barriers which have stifled productive sharing will assure improvement in children's lives. The investments demanded of the various populations are surely worthy.

Glossary

Achievement level: Expected grade level minus actual achievement grade level; the distance in months and years a child is behind his average peers in the same grade.

Affect: Mental processes involving moods, emotions, and feelings.

    (a) LIGHT AFFECT—a state characterized by well-developed social skills and good interpersonal relationships.

    (b) DULL AFFECT—a state characterized by withdrawad, retarded social development, depressed speech, and inadequate display of emotion.

    (c) INAPPROPRIATE AFFECT—the display of affect or emotion which is inconsistent with the situation such as exhibiting laughter in unhappy circumstances.

Affective responses: A term used to describe the display of feeling, emotion, and temperament.

Akinesis: The absence of intentional movement due to paralysis, neuroticism, or intense pain.

Antisocial behavior: Offensive behavior characterized by deliberateness, an understanding of the consequences of the behavior, and lack of remorse.

Anxiety: A feeling of uneasiness or dread without specific cause, usually accompanied by physical symptoms such as increased heart rate, dryness of the mouth, body tremors, etc.

Approach-approach dichotomy: A state in which the individual is forced to choose between two attractive but incompatible goals.

Approach-avoidance dichotomy: A state in which a goal has both attracting and repelling characteristics.

Associated movements: Irrelevant muscular movements accompanying purposeful motor activity.

Atonia: The absence of regular muscular tone and strength.

Auditory closure: The ability to recognize the whole from a partially presented auditory stimulus.

Auditory localization: The ability to focus and identify characteristics of auditory stimuli.

Auditory recognition: The ability to understand and interpret auditory material.

Auditory sequential memory: The ability to recall a sequence of auditory material.

Avoidance-avoidance dichotomy: A state in which the individual is forced to choose between two equally repelling goals.

Body image: Perception of one's physical body.

Brain dysfunction: A medical designation for abnormalities of behavior and/or intellectual functioning which result from a central nervous system and/or developmental dysfunction. Note that the term does not imply damage but emphasizes dysfunctioning.

Cognitive flow: Refers to the type and quality of thought expression revealed during a child's verbal communication.

Cognitive map structure: The formation of mental blueprints used in making a response to a situation.

Conduct disorders: Antisocial activities which interfere with behaviors of other individuals and society. Children with these disorders make others the victim of their psychological conflicts.

Conversion reactions: Physical complaints such as blindness, paralysis, enuresis, deafness, headaches, etc. due to underlying emotional conflict.

Cooperative play: Play characterized by interacting, sharing, and experiencing with others.

Curiosity-exploratory behavior: A tendency to seek knowledge and experience by investigating and becoming involved in new and novel circumstances.

Cyanosis: A bluish discoloration of the face and skin, resulting from imperfectly oxygenated blood.

Cyclothymic mood changes: The tendency to alternate between excitement and depression.

Decoding: The process by which a receiver translates signals into messages, as in reading.

Delusional ideations: False ideas and beliefs, usually unmodifiable by reason.

(a) DELUSIONS OF GRANDEUR—adopting character of a great or powerful person for the purpose of elevating one's own worth.

(b) DELUSIONS OF PERSECUTION—a false belief that one is the object of others' efforts to cause injury or harm.

Developmental spiral: The child takes two maturational steps forward and one backward. The backward regression apparently reflects consolidation of previous maturational growth.

Directionality: A child's perception of an object's relationship to another object or point in space. Left-right confusion may result from difficulty with this skill.

Dyscalcula: The inability to perform mathematical functions.

Dysgraphia: The lack of ability to initiate fine motor movements necessary for writing letters or numbers.

Dyslexia: An impairment of the ability to attain reading skills.

Dysnomia: The lack of ability to consistently recall or remember names of objects or words.

Encoding: The process of expressing knowledge through written, oral, or body language.

Encopresis: Involuntary discharge of feces.

Enuresis: Involuntary discharge of urine.

(a) CHRONIC ENURESIS—never obtained bladder control.

(b) DIURNAL ENURESIS—daytime enuresis.

(c) NOCTURAL ENURESIS—nighttime enuresis.

(d) ORGANIC ENURESIS—enuresis with an underlying physical basis.

(e) REGRESSIVE ENURESIS—loss of bladder control after it has been obtained.

Expressive language: The process of communicating through verbalization, writing, and gestures.

Fantasy: The extravagant, unrestrained process of imagining in which desires are fulfilled.

(a) CREATIVE FANTASY—the process by which a child originates novel and productive thought and expression through imagery; a healthy process.

(b) WITHDAWAL FANTASY—the process by which a child retreats and ruminates imaginary events to the preference of reality contact; an unhealthy process.

Faulty social perception: Inappropriate interpretation of social cues and events characterized by persistence in committing the offensive behavior.

Fecal mass: Discharge of excrement.

Focal motor seizure: An epileptic seizure characterized by convulsions of a limited body area associated with retention of consciousness.

Fugue states: Brief lapses of consciousness with no recollection of their occurrence.

Functional: A learned psychological reaction as opposed to one which developed from an organic etiology.

Genitourinary anomalies: Medical abnormalities of the genital and urinary organs.

Grand mal seizure: A disorder of the nervous system characterized by prolonged loss of consciousness, motor control, and severe convulsions.

Hallucination: False perceptions of sensations in the various sensory modalities.

(a) AUDITORY SENSORY DISTORTIONS—experiencing imaginary voices without the presence of another person.

(b) VISUAL SENSORY DISORTIONS—experiencing visual images in the absence of a physical stimulus.

(c) KINESTHETIC SENSORY DISTORTIONS—experiencing tactile or muscular sensations in the absence of a physical stimulus.

Hyperkinesia: Heightened motor and/or verbal activity.

Hypochondriacal reactions: Excessive concern about one's health, usually accompanied by anxiety and depression.

Intracranial neoplasm: New or abnormal growth, such as a tumor, located within the cranium.

Intrapsychic disorder: Emotional tension produced by conflicts within the child as opposed to those originated from their peer group or external to the individual.

Jacksonian seizure: An epileptic seizure which involves involuntary progressive convulsive movement of the muscles while the patient retains consciousness.

Kinesthesia: The awareness and adjustment to the environment by body movement through muscular feedback.

Laterality: The preferential use of one side of the body, especially in tasks demanding the use of only one hand, one eye, or one foot.

Maladaptation: Inability to adapt one's behavior to the conditions of his environment; it is sometimes referred to as maladjustment.

Manic depression states: A severe mental disorder characterized by shifts in mood from elation to depression.

Mirror movements: Motor activity which occurs simultaneous to the purposeful activity on opposite side of the body.

Mixed dominance: The failure of one side of the brain to be clearly dominant over the other in motor control. The resulting conflict is held to be the cause of speech and perceptual deficits.

Multisensory approaches: Educational techniques which require the use of several sensory modalities used simultaneously or individually to facilitate learning.

Neologisms: The coining of new words and different meanings of words.

Nonperipheral impairment: Impairments that are not contained in the sensory modalities but occur within the central nervous system.

Nonverbal neurogenic learning disabilities: The child's inability to understand and comprehend the body language of others. *Neurogenic* refers to the inability to process nonverbal information and it is synonymous with social misperception.

Objective anxiety: A feeling of uneasiness or dread for which there is an identifiable cause.

Parallel play: A type of play between the ages of 18 and 24 months, where children play side by side but without social interaction.

Parataxic mode of experiencing: Characterized by abnormalities in thinking which result from ideas or attitudes that are not logically integrated into the thinking processes.

Pathognomonic: Characteristic of a disease; a sign or symptom from which a diagnosis can be made.

Perseveration: Continuation of activity after the initiating stimulus has ceased.

Personality disorders: Items which reflect intrapsychic features with the child himself being the victim of his own psychological conflicts.

Pervasive anxiety: An overwhelming and continuous state of tension and anxiety.

Petit mal seizure: A form of epilepsy in which there is a brief lapse of consciousness; it is sometimes referred to as an absence attack. It is usually seen in children and may occur many times daily.

Phobic reaction: An excessive fear of a specific object, event, or situation.

Psychoanalysis: A theory directed toward the understanding, cure, and prevention of mental disorders developed by Sigmund Freud.

Psychogenic: Disorders originating psychologically as opposed to disorders originating from an organic basis.

Psychomotor seizure: An epileptic disorder characterized by motor and/or verbal activity which is inappropriate for the time and place and about which the subject has no memory following the seizure.

Psychosexual: Refers to the emotional development of sexuality, pertaining to sexuality in its broadest sense, including both mental and physical affects.

Psychosis: A severe mental disorder characterized by disorganized thought, loss of contact with reality, disorientation, hallucinations, delusions, and disturbances in emotional stability.

Receptive language: The ability to receive, understand, and gain meaningfulness of language which is communicated by speech or written means.

Rumination: The process of concentrating and pondering events for an unusually long time period.

School diagnostician: Refers to any school personnel who specializes in diagnosing exceptional behaviors related to learning, emotional, and social aspects of children such as a school psychologist, counselor, psychometrist, educational strategist, etc.

Secondary reinforcer: A learned reinforcement.

Self-concept: An individual's thoughts about his physical, cognitive, social, and emotional capacities.

Soft neurological signs: Subtle and minimal deficiencies in fine-gross motor coordination and perceptual-motor integration.

Solitary play: A type of play where the child occupies himself with bouncing, squirming, pulling, and other activities and does not require the interaction of children and/or adults. It usually characterizes children below 18 months of age.

Somatic symptoms: Organic or physical symptoms as opposed to mental or psychological disorders.

Superstitious behavior: A tendency to assign cause-and-effect relationships because of faulty association.

Tic: A spasmodic or sudden twitch, usually of one of the face or head muscles, which results from excessive anxiety.

Trauma: A sudden negative experience and/or shock, producing sustained and lasting emotional or psychological effects for the individual.

Urticaria: A vascular reaction of the skin marked by the transient appearance of smooth, slightly elevated patches, which are redder or paler than the surrounding skin and often attended by severe itching.

Visual closure: The ability to recognize the whole from a partially presented visual stimulus.

Visual figure-ground: The ability to attend to foreground visual stimuli against irrelevant background visual stimuli.

Visual sequential memory: The ability to recall a sequence of visually presented stimuli.

Visual recognition: The ability to interpret visually presented material.

References

American Psychiatric Association: *Diagnostic and Statistical Manual of Mental Disorders*. Washington, D.C., American Psychiatric Association, 1968.

Arieti, S.: *Interpretation of Schizophrenia*. New York, Robert Brunner, 1955.

Axline, V. M.: *DIBS in Search of Self*. New York, Ballantine Books, 1964.

Bakwin, H.: Suicide in children and adolescents. *Journal of Pediatrics, 50:* 749-769, 1957.

Beilin, H.: Teacher's and clinician attitudes toward the behavior of children, a reappraisal. *Child Development, 30:*9-25, 1959.

Branan, J. M.: Negative human interaction. *Journal of Counseling Psychology, 19(1):*81-82, 1972.

Bridge, E. M.: *Epilepsy and Convulsive Disorders in Children*. New York, McGraw-Hill, 1949.

Bridges, K. M. B.: Emotional development in early infancy. *Child Development, 3:*324-341, 1932.

Burks, H. F.: *Burks' Behavior Rating Scales*. Huntington Beach, California, Arden Press, 1968.

Burks, H. F.: The hyperkinetic child. *Exceptional Children, 27:*18-26, 1950.

Charlton, M. H.: Minimal brain dysfunction and the hyperkinetic child. *New York State Journal of Medicine, 2058:* 1972.

Clements, S. D.: *Minimal brain dysfunction in children* (NINDS Monograph No. 3, U.S. Public Health Service Publication No. 1415). Washington, D.C., U.S. Government Printing Office, 1966.

Conners, C. K.: A teacher rating scale for use in drug studies with children. *American Journal of Psychiatry, 126:*152, 1969.

Coopersmith, S.: Self-esteem and need achievement as determinants of selective recall and repetition. *Journal of Abnormal and Social Psychology, 60:*310-317, 1960.

Denenberg, V. H., and Bell, R. W.: Critical periods for the effects of infantile experience on adult learning. *Science, 131:*1960.

Doll, E. A. Vineland Social Maturity Scale. Circle Pines, Minn.: American Guidance Services, Inc., 1965.

Dmitriev, V.: Motor and cognitive development in early education. In N. Haring (Ed.): *Behavior of Exceptional Children—an Introduction to Special Education*. Columbus, Ohio, Charles E. Merrill Publishing Co., 1974.

Elkind, D. A.: *Sympathetic Understanding of the Child Six to Sixteen.* Boston, Allyn & Bacon, 1971.

English, H. B., and English, A. C.: *A Comprehensive Dictionary of Psychological and Psychoanalytical Terms.* New York, Longmans Green, 1958.

Erikson, E. H.: *Childhood and Society,* 2nd ed. New York, W. W. Norton, 1963.

Eysenck, H. J., and Rachman, S.: *The Causes and Cures of Neurosis.* San Diego, Robert R. Knapp, 1965.

Finch, S. M.: *Fundamentals of Child Psychiatry.* New York, W. W. Norton, 1960.

Fremont, T., Klingsporn, J., and Wilson, J.: Identifying emotional disturbance—The professionals differ. *Journal of School Psychology,* in press.

Freud, S.: *An Outline of Psychoanalysis.* New York, Norton, 1949.

Freud, S.: *Collected Papers.* New York, Basic Books, 1959.

Friedman, A. P., and Harms, E.: *Headaches in Children.* Springfield, Illinois, Charles C Thomas, 1967.

Garrand, S. P., and Richamond, J. B.: Psychogenic megacolon manifesting by fecal soiling. *Pediatrics, 10*:474, 1952.

Gauron, E.: Infantile shock traumatization and subsequent adaptibility to stress. *Journal of Genetic Psychology, 104*:167-178, 1964.

Gearheart, B. R.: *Education of the Exceptional Child: History, Present Practices, and Trends.* San Francisco, California, International Textbook Company, 1972.

Gesell, A., and Ilg, F.: *Child Development.* New York, Harper and Row, 1949.

Greenberg, J.: *I Never Promised You a Rose Garden.* New York, Holt, Rinehart & Winston, 1964.

Harriman, P. L.: *Handbook of Psychological Terms.* New Jersey, Littlefield, Adams & Co., 1965.

Harris, A.: *Harris Test of Lateral Dominance,* ref. ed. New York, Psychological Corporation, 1958.

Heinstein, M.: *Child Rearing in California.* Berkeley, California, Bureau of Maternal and Child Health, Department of Public Health, State of California, 1966.

Hill, K. T., and Sarason, S. B.: The relation of test anxiety and defensiveness to test and school performance over the elementary school years: a further longitudinal study. *Society for Research in Child Development, 31*, (serial no. 104), 1966.

Homan, W. E.: *Child Sense.* New York, Basic Books, Inc., 1969.

Horney, K.: *The Neurotic Personality of Our Time.* New York, W. W. Norton, 1937.

Hurlock, B.: *Child Growth and Development.* St. Louis, McGraw-Hill, 1968.

Hutt, L., and Gibby, R.: *The Child: Development and Adjustment*. Boston, Allyn and Bacon, 1959.

Jenkins, R. L.: Diagnostic classification in child psychiatry. *American Journal of Psychiatry, 127*:680-681, 1970.

Jung, C. G.: *The Psychology of Dementia Praecox*. New York, Nervous and Mental Disease Publishing Co., 1936.

Kanner, L.: Infantile autism and the schizophrenias. *Behavioral Science, 10*:412-420, 1965.

Keagn, B. K.: Hyperactivity and learning problems: implications for teachers. *Academic Therapy, 7*:47-50, 1971.

Keith, H. M.: *Convulsive Disorders in Children*. Boston, Little, Brown, 1963.

Kelly, E. W.: School phobia: a review of theory and treatment. *Psychology in the Schools, 10*:33-42, 1973.

Ketal, R.: Affect, mood, emotion and feeling: Semantic considerations. *American Journal of Psychiatry, 132*:11, 1215-1217, 1975.

Koos, E. M.: Manifestations of cerebral dominance and reading retardation in primary-grade children. *Journal of Genetic Psychology, 104*:155-166, 1964.

Lerner, J. W.: *Children with Learning Disabilities—Theories, Diagnosis, and Teaching Strategies*. Boston, Houghton Mifflin Co., 1971.

Levinson, B.: Understanding the child with school phobia. *Exceptional Children, 28*:393-397, 1962.

Lewin, K.: *A Dynamic Theory of Personality*. New York, McGraw-Hill, 1935.

Mattsson, A.: Suicidal behavior as a child psychiatric emergency. *Archives of General Psychiatry, 20*:100-109, 1969.

Miller, L., Barrett, C., and Hempe, E.: Phobias of childhood in a prescientific era. In Davis, A. (Ed.): *Child Personality and Psychopathology*. New York, John Wiley & Sons, 1974, pp. 89-134.

Myklebust, H. R.: *The Pupil Rating Scale*. New York, Grune & Stratton, 1971.

Nagy, M. H.: The child's view of death. In Feifel, H. (Ed.): *The Meaning of Death*. New York, McGraw-Hill, 1959.

Peterson, D. R.: Behavior patterns of middle childhood. *Journal of Consulting Psychology, 25*:205-209, 1961.

Pierce, C. M.: Enuresis. In Freedman, A. M., and Kaplan, H. I. (Eds.): *Comprehensive Textbook of Psychiatry*. Baltimore, Williams & Wilkins Co., 1967.

Pierce, C. M., Whitman, R. R., Maas, J. W., and Gay, M. I.: Enuresis and dreaming. *Archives of General Psychiatry, 4*:166-170, 1961.

Pinkerton, P.: Psychogenic megacolon in children: the implications of bowel negativism. *Archives of Disease in Childhood, 33*:371, 1958.

Robins, L. N.: *Deviant Children Grown Up: A Sociological and Psychiatric Study of Sociopathic Personality.* Baltimore, Williams & Wilkins Co., 1966.

Rodin, E. A.: *The Prognosis of Patients with Epilepsy.* Springfield, Illinois, Charles C Thomas, 196

Ross, O. A.: Learning difficulties of children: Dysfunctions, disorders, disabilities. *Journal of School Psychology, 5:*82-92, 1967.

Rutter, M., and Bartak, L.: Causes of infantile autism: some considerations from recent research. *Journal of Autism and Childhood Schizophrenia, 1:*20-32, 1971.

Schuyler, D.: When was the last time you took a suicidal child to lunch? *Journal of School Health, 43:*504-506, 1973.

Sears, R. R., Maccoby, E. E., and Levin, H.: *Patterns of Childrearing.* Evanston, Illinois, Row, Peterson & Co., 1957.

Siegel, E.: *The Exceptional Child Grows Up.* New York, E. P. Dutton, 1974.

Spivack, G., Haimes, P. E., and Spotts, J.: *Devereux Adolescent Behavior Rating Scale Manual.* Devon, Pennsylvania, The Devereux Foundation, 1967.

Spivack, G., and Swift, M.: *Devereux Elementary School Behavior Rating Scale Manual.* Devon, Pennsylvania, The Devereux Foundation, 1967.

Stengel, E.: Definition and classification of suicidal acts. In Litman, R. E. (Ed.): *Proceedings, Sixth International Conference for Suicide Prevention.* Ann Arbor, Edward Brothers, Inc., 1972.

Stewart, M.: Hyperactive children. *Scientific American,* 94-98, 1970.

Sullivan, H. S.: *The Interpersonal Theory of Psychiatry.* New York, W. W. Norton, 1953.

Tietz, W.: School phobia and the fear of death. *Mental Hygiene, 54:*565-568, 1970.

Walsh, A. M.: *Self-Concepts of Bright Boys with Learning Difficulties.* New York, Teachers College Press, 1956.

Walsh, J. F., and O'Conner, J. D.: When are children disturbed? *Elementary School Journal, 68:*353-356, 1968.

Wichita Guidance Center: Interview Form for Children. Wichita, Kansas, unpublished.

Wickman, E. K.: *Children's Behavior and Teacher's Attitudes.* New York, Commonwealth Fund Division of Publications, 1928.

Williams, C. D.: Case report: the elimination of tantrum behavior by extinction procedures. *Journal of Abnormal and Social Psychology, 59:* 269, 1959.

Index